HAUNTED

E. JAY GILBERT

Dr E. Jay Gilbert is a writer, academic and researcher based in Oxford, originally from the north-east of England. She has an MA and MSt from the University of Oxford and a PhD from the University of Leicester and is a lecturer in Applied Linguistics at The Open University. She currently co-edits *The Banshee*, a women's literary journal with a particular focus on the supernatural.

HAUNTED

E. JAY GILBERT

MANILLA
PRESS

First published in the UK in 2024 by
MANILLA PRESS
An imprint of Zaffre Publishing Group
A Bonnier Books UK Company
4th Floor, Victoria House, Bloomsbury Square, London WC1B 4DA
Owned by Bonnier Books
Sveavägen 56, Stockholm, Sweden

A CIP catalogue record for this book
is available from the British Library.

Hardback ISBN: 978-1-78658-291-1
Trade Paperback ISBN: 978-1-78658-289-8

Also available as an ebook and an audiobook

1 3 5 7 9 10 8 6 4 2

Typeset by IDSUK (Data Connection) Ltd
Printed and bound in Great Britain by Clays Ltd, Elcograf S.p.A.

FSC
www.fsc.org
MIX
Paper | Supporting
responsible forestry
FSC® C018072

Manilla Press is an imprint of Zaffre Publishing Group
A Bonnier Books UK company
www.bonnierbooks.co.uk

For Dad, who taught me to love stories;
Mam, who taught me to believe; and
Nanna, who is always with me.
All my love from your Em

Contents

Introduction

ONE SODDEN NOVEMBER EVENING in 1950, a man pulled up outside The Scrogg pub in Byker, an electoral ward of Newcastle upon Tyne now known to many of us via children's TV classic, *Byker Grove*, but which was then a post-Victorian estate due for demolition. It was, quite literally, a dark and stormy night. Thunder crashed overhead at ear-splitting volume, and the rain that had been falling steadily since five had turned abruptly into an intense downpour that seemed to rush at the car from all directions. The man, not local, was lost. It was still possible to be lost in those days, before sat navs and Google Maps had been developed to get in the way of travellers' tales. The pub was closed, but the man could see a light still aglow in a downstairs window. Braving the rain, he drew up the collar of his overcoat and thumped on the door with a closed fist.

A female voice called out through the door, informing him that the pub was shut and that everyone had gone home. The man persisted: 'I'm lost. Can I use your loo and get my bearings?'

A brief silence. The man was well-spoken, 'posh' by Byker standards, and that seemed to make an impression on the young woman who, after a moment's hesitation, opened the door. She was dark haired, slim as a blade in her apron. There was nothing to suggest she'd borne two children already, a war bride like so many others. The man craned his neck to look past her and saw a second girl, the pair of them obviously cleaning up after a night spent fielding dockyard-hands and drunkards.

Two people in the pub, then, he thought.

Of course, he was wrong. This is a ghost story.

The man thanked the two cleaners and followed their directions to the gents'. Thirty seconds later he was back, wild-eyed, his flies undone. 'I thought you said you were closed?' he said, high-pitched and harried.

The girls laughed. The dark-haired one was called Polly and she was my grandmother. This was one of her stories. She died in 1999, but the story rumbles dutifully on.

'There's a bloke in the loos,' said the man. 'Either you've missed a punter, or someone's broken in!'

'Oh, that's just Charlie,' Polly told him. 'Don't mind him!'

The man minded. He left apace, without having found either his bearings or his equilibrium.

This particular visitor, discombobulated and out of his element, didn't stop to tell Polly what he had seen in the gents' – but he didn't need to. Polly had heard the story many times before. One moment, the loos would be empty of everything but a row of urinals and a stale smell. Then, a customer going about his business would look up to see an old man in the corner, wearing an overcoat and flat cap, grey-faced, watching. His stare was intense and disconcerting. If the customer spoke, his ensuing silence was more disturbing still, setting the hairs prickling on the nape of the neck. Nobody likes to enter an empty room by its only door and then look up to meet the unwavering gaze of a man who, most definitely, had not been there a second before. Most people would beat an understandably hasty retreat.

Charlie didn't keep the factory-men and ship-workers out of The Scrogg, but he stopped them lingering in the loos, especially after closing time. They were nothing to Charlie, undeserving even of a flicker of interest, but he remained a permanent, unsettling fact of life for them.

The thing is this: ghost stories aren't just about ghosts. We don't know who Charlie was, or why he walked around The Scrogg at night after everyone else had left. Sometimes, on television, they tie these things up neatly. Charlie would have a tragic backstory, or unfinished business. Charlie's bones would be secreted in the basement, crying out for justice. In real life, though, it doesn't necessarily matter who Charlie was. He wasn't even really called Charlie, unless through absolute and unprovable coincidence. 'Charlie' was what Polly called him when she was cleaning up and heard footsteps overhead. Her sister Meg once went fearlessly upstairs to the room where Charlie was. It was empty, of course. Below, Polly tapped at the ceiling with a broom handle every time she heard a step, and Meg upstairs said, 'No, no, there's nothing here.'

There's no great reveal to this story; no grand denouement. Charlie's identity and motivations remain a mystery, but this hasn't stopped the story being repeated for seventy years. Charlie himself – whoever he may have been, and why he was there – isn't primarily what we're interested in when we want to hear about ghosts. The story is about Polly, and the unnamed man, and how it felt to hear Charlie every night. The story is about the experience.

The north-east of England, the place of my birth, is sometimes called the Land of Castles or, more romantically, the Secret Kingdom. Many of its fortified stately homes and stark-faced bastle houses, representing the legacy of the borderlands as an embattled no-go area between two kingdoms, are now owned by English Heritage and the National Trust. Others, notably Chillingham Castle, near Alnwick, remain in private hands, with the result that one can dubiously pass an afternoon peering into rooms inexplicably filled with boots, or reviewing records of the owner's history of amateur aviation. Once-grand houses of this ilk exist, of course, all over the country in shocking numbers. What all these ancestral piles have in common, whatever their current ownership, is that they are – legend has it – riddled with ghosts. Moreover, whoever is in charge of their marketing material has been informed that ghosts are the new sex. Ghosts sell.

So, then: the promotional leaflets and the pamphlets list every white lady and inexplicably blue boy who's ever been whispered about in the history of the place in question. At Chillingham Castle, ghost tourism is booming business. The lake at Chillingham reportedly turns red at certain moments, recalling the blood of Scottish soldiers slaughtered there in centuries past. Certainly a site of much historic mystery and mayhem, ghost tours, ghost hunts, and 'vigils' are run here year round – at prices which keep pace with inflation, of course. The castle website notes that a 'frail figure in white' appears in the inner pantry, while in the chapel, the voices of two men are 'often heard' but peter out whenever anyone pays too much attention. But the real question is: to *whom* has this figure in white appeared, and when?

Pushing aside the all-too-common passive voice, who has heard the two men conversing in the chapel, and what do they talk about? A list of rumoured ghosts is all well and good, but what we really want are the personal accounts of those to whom these ghosts have appeared. We want first-hand stories; we want to know the way it felt to have the hairs rise silently on the back of the neck at the sudden sound of a man's voice in an empty pantry. For many readers and listeners, our interest is not hugely affected by whether or not we know the 'true' identity of a spirit. We're far more concerned with what, *exactly,* the spirit did or said, and what the witness thought of it. We are interested in the encounter.

In these days of declining church attendance and diminishing superstition, we might expect interest in the supernatural to be declining, too. The world is becoming ever smaller, after all, and science is increasingly draining the mystery from what once was magic. And yet, we have only to scan the top ten podcasts on Spotify to see that this isn't true. Almost everyone, I've found, has a ghost story – which, depending on where we're from and how we were raised, we might be willing to tell with more or fewer caveats, greater or less conviction. The same stories, up and down the country, recur in different forms, passed on from generation to generation. Why, I wonder, are we still so captivated by the concept of the supernatural? What do our spectres tell us about ourselves? What are the things that haunt us – and why can't we seem to shake our belief in them?

*

When I was eighteen, I came to Oxford to take up a university place. Oxford, I'm told, is a deeply haunted city. This is not something I have learned through any first-hand experience, but rather because, even in 2020, in the midst of the coronavirus pandemic, the placards spreading the word of the 'Ghost Tour' retained their pride of place on Broad Street, outside Balliol College where the Gunpowder Plot was hatched. As soon as government restrictions were lifted sufficiently to make it legal, the (socially distant, number-restricted) ghost tours resumed, promising 'demons and death', 'sinister spirits' and, lest we forget ourselves, a 'health warning'. Forget the pandemic: it's the 'post-tour complications' that might get you. Ghost walks are an essential business.

The thing is, ghosts are experienced differently in a place like Oxford to the way they are in small towns and rural fringes where nary a coachload of tourists would ever think to stop. Ghost tourism may rake in the big bucks all over the country, but where Oxford's story is peopled with the lofty likes of Charles I, Oscar Wilde and prominent royalists such as Colonel Francis Windebank, the ghosts of obscure stately homes and run-down borderland castles are less notable figures, largely being nameless nuns, minor aristocrats and fabled walled-up children. More importantly, the ghosts of somewhere little-peopled, little-visited and little-remarked-upon are more likely to be truly believed in. In a tourist town with a rich history, ghost tours are entertainment: the more celebrities, the better. Elsewhere, the names are less important; the tropes – the white lady; the blue boy – more so. Outside of the castles – in the pubs, the schools, the hospitals – are the ghosts who make their way into family stories, to be told over Sunday dinner for decades to come. These are the spirits whispered about at primary schools and playgroups, at the hairdresser's and at the dentist. We often don't know the origins of the stories, or who the spirits supposedly were in life. We rarely care. We only want to know what Mary's mother's auntie saw in the attic of that house that's been sold nine times in as many years.

In 2017, a survey was conducted by statista.com, asking UK citizens whether they believed in the paranormal. The outcome suggested that 33 per cent of UK adults were willing to admit to a belief in 'ghosts, ghouls, spirits or other types of paranormal activity'. A similar survey conducted by Newcastle's flagship newspaper, *The Evening Chronicle*, however, reported the greatly elevated figure of 67 per cent of adults believing in the paranormal in the North-East. When I mentioned this discrepancy to a Welsh friend, he observed that it was potentially a trait of the Celtic fringes and other isolated cultural pockets – an idea supported by a perusal of various regional newspapers, which indicates that many rural areas, such as Cornwall and North Yorkshire, accept the potential for the paranormal at similar rates. Whatever the reason, evidence suggests that while in some parts of the country, belief in the supernatural would be a foolish thing to admit to in public, in other places the attitude is both more open-minded and more pragmatic: the supernatural is not exactly commonplace, but it is an accepted possibility. This attitude can be found the whole world over, especially in more rural areas, and interestingly, the same spectres seem to reappear in different places, their context altered but their characters largely unchanged. It seems we all know the same ghosts: it's simply a question of how doggedly they haunt us.

*

As a child, I went for my six-monthly dental appointments in an old Victorian house, four storeys tall, which had been converted into a surgery. It stood at the top of a ludicrously steep hill which set cars grinding at the best of times and which became completely impassable in wintry weather. The dentist's surgery, despite its ornate bannisters and curious alcoves, wasn't haunted. The house opposite, however, was.

Everybody knew about The House. Whenever I got out of the car in anticipation of a ritual teeth-scraping, one of my parents would point it out: The Haunted House. I saw it listed on a property website a few months ago, being sold for the third time in as many years. It was gorgeous, lavishly decorated and beautifully restored. It was also being sold at something far below the market rate, even for the North-East, whose house prices can usually make southerners weep with envy. Once a house has a reputation, it can be difficult to shake. For example, in the notorious 'Ghostbusters' case of *Stambovsky vs Ackley* from 1991, a house in Nyack, New York, was ruled to be 'legally haunted'; because its owner, Helen Ackley, had disclosed its poltergeist activity in national publications, she was thereafter legally obligated to inform all potential purchasers about the spectral squatters.

Nobody who lived in The House in Elspeth Street, Blaydon[1] had ever given so much as an interview to the local newspaper, and yet word of the ghosts travelled fast

---

[1] Like many names in this book, this is a pseudonym – but locals will well know the street's real name.

enough by mouth. Seeing this listing again brought me to a sudden realisation. I knew that The House was haunted. I had heard it muttered about for years as yet another family moved in, dismissive of the rumours and eager for a bargain, and then, inevitably, moved out again, quietly, as if in disgrace. But I didn't know what form those hauntings supposedly took. I didn't know *what happened,* and why it was awful enough (or insidious enough, or relentless enough) to force a swift sale. And that, after all, is what we always want to know.

On the one hand, this curiosity seems almost callous – for these people, the haunting has had a serious impact on their lives and probably their finances. But the urge to tell scary stories, to hear them from the mouths of someone we know and trust, is an old one, and oddly irresistible. We don't have to know who the spirit is, or how he or she met a tragic demise. What we really want is the illicit thrill of hearing how a real, down-to-earth person like us, saw a dark figure pass by in the hallway, or heard a whispered voice in the dark. The Victorians understood it best: the greatest ghost stories aren't the ones that can be tied up neatly, but those which, like the horrifying bedsheet-spectre in M. R. James's classic, 'Oh, Whistle and I'll Come To You, My Lad', simply unravel into nothingness, leaving behind an electric shiver and a sense of unease. The inexplicable, the incongruous, the impossible – these are the elements which resonate for years after a sighting. When a ghost story is explained, the ghost is, in a sense, laid to rest. But the figures who hover in stairwells, appear impossibly in the windows of closed-off attics, and vanish without explanation – these are the ones which walk our mental landscapes forever, throwing up unanswerable questions as we try to fall asleep at night.

I began researching this book because I wanted the thrill of finally hearing what residents had experienced in The House. I continued writing it because, for every person who had a genuine insight into the story of that house, there were four or five with different, complementary stories, and the patterns that began to emerge intrigued me. Some of the storytellers had either been, or been closely acquainted with, former inhabitants of The House, but the stories had spread and warped far beyond these close circles, a chaotic tapestry woven by many hands. People wanted to believe in the ghost of Elspeth Street. They wanted to get to the heart of the mystery, become part of it – but at the same time, to preserve its intrigue. They preferred to luxuriate in the eeriness, spinning the story outward and outward in concentric circles. I could relate to this. I have always, more or less, accepted the supernatural as a fact of life, but I don't know how it feels to sleep in a room I'm convinced is haunted. What must it be like to confront a spectral face from another century and step out of the twilight of belief into the spotlight of *knowing?* I, like many others, am fascinated and horrified by this concept.

How many of our friends and neighbours, do you think, have had a paranormal experience? As I researched this book, I found that people across the whole of the UK had countless stories to tell – from wettest Wales to darkest Dorset; the rolling Dales to the banks of Loch Lomond. Perhaps most people have simply never been asked to tell the stories you couldn't put in a guidebook or a whimsical local history – the tales of haunted hairdresser's and bumps on the night bus; the mundane and myriad spirits in local schools, hospitals and nursing homes. Perhaps most people, as the statistics suggest, are reluctant to admit that they believe, until asked directly. As I considered what local incarnations of spectral tropes could tell us about the communities that shaped them, it became increasingly clear that tracking these patterns across the wider British Isles was the way to truly see what's written in the stones.

*

In one sense, the stories in this book could have taken place anywhere. That is the joy of them. The White Lady of Gibside Hall may be a close relative of the figure in white seen at neighbouring Chillingham, or the White Woman of Shepton Mallet Prison, but she also finds analogues in the Brazilian *Dama Branca,* the Dutch *witte wieven,* and *La Llorona* of Mexico, all female spirits characterised by betrayal and loss. The *Barghest* spirits of Yorkshire and Northumberland, which haunt churchyards in the form of large black dogs, are akin to the Welsh *Gwyllgi*, the Flemish *Oude Rode Ogen,* and the Central American *Cadejo.* The universality of certain castes and categories of spectral encounters is both well-documented

12

and fascinating. From black dogs to Bloody Mary, in a community of believers, there is rarely a ghost without parallel.

At one point, having watched a series of Japanese horror films back to back, I noted the unifying theme of revenge-ghosts, or *yūrei,* being interpreted as an irritating but inevitable pest, like rats or feral youth. There's always a long-suffering police detective poised to fish an incriminating long dark hair out of a drain: ah, yes. Another case of *yūrei.* Clearly, though, the same sort of thinking – the instant attribution of minor irritations to supernatural causes – went through the minds of the more than eighty people who contacted police forces in England between 2008 and 2012 to complain about supernatural disturbances. In 2009, Northumberland Police received a call from one man who claimed that he could see 'eight witches' on his roof, a self-evidently unacceptable situation which he felt they should do something about. Numerous others across Yorkshire, Cumbria, North Wales and East Anglia chose the police as their first port of call when they became aware of a home invader of the less corporeal sort, with one local medium suggesting that most approached police forces even before trying their luck with a priest. (Of course, the medium was dismissive of both, seeming to view herself as a sort of paranormal clean-up operation who regularly succeeded where the law and the church failed: 'I come in and get rid of everything'.)

The usefulness and proper application of the police is a topic that has recently been under much discussion, but rarely has the accusation been levelled against them that they ought to provide a more efficient ghost-busting service. Still, the facts – come by honestly, through the medium (no pun intended) of a Freedom of Information Request – speak for themselves: in the minds of many, a ghost infestation is a very real problem that requires a real and tangible solution.

The thing is, of course, that while Gibside's White Lady may have spiritual cousins all over the world, the way she is understood and appreciated has its roots in the community and context that birthed and sustains her. The same is true of the White Lady of St Michael's Mount, or Y Ladi Wen of Carew Castle. All ghosts are like this. While our love of Ghost Trouble may be universal, our ghosts themselves are specific and local, growing out of and feeding back into our communities. To grow up in a post-industrial mining area, where spiritualist churches and social clubs stand side by side, is to grow up haunted. This is true in a social and political sense: the resonating echoes of heavy industry can be heard all over the UK, in places which thrived in the industrial age and have been haunted ever since by its passing. For many of us – still, and sometimes more than ever – ghosts are as much an accepted fact of life as the living family next door.

This book is about the ghosts that haunt communities, on community levels – the house guests, the local legends, the witches. But it is also about the wider questions: must a haunting be verifiable to have an observable effect? How does a community shape the reception and the proliferation of its own ghosts? And why are the ghosts of the British Isles so reliably mappable onto similar spectres from Belgium to Brazil, Newfoundland to the Netherlands? What universal chords do these particularly prevalent manifestations strike? I have always been fascinated by the supernatural, not least because of the nonchalant way in which local hauntings were often discussed in my childhood. In a world where podcasts like *Uncanny* are surging in popularity, and infrared ghost-hunting has been a staple of Saturday night cable television for years, it is clear I'm far from alone. Life is changing quickly, and in the past century has changed with greater rapidity than at any other point in history. Paranormal belief, however, clearly hasn't been a casualty of that change. As is evidenced by the unstoppable rise of horror content in all its forms, we still want to wallow in vicarious thrills and terrors, the promise of the unknown. Very well, then. Let's do it.

This book takes as its frame the categories of ghost stories which appeared most frequently in my research, leading the reader on a ghost tour which explores the echoes in the churchyard, the whispers by the water and the shadows in the forest. But the communities that form the settings for these stories are only the avatar for thousands of similar communities the world over, each of which will have its own uncharted instances of the uncanny, and its own contextual impact on the archetypes with which we are all familiar. I began writing because of my dogged interest in a particular haunted house, but in the end, what I have written is an exploration of the ghosts within British communities and within ourselves, and why they are so compelling and so context-bound, even while they are frequently archetypal.

Some of the stories in this book were told to me first-hand – by friends, family members and colleagues; by strangers in pubs and on message boards. Others were shared second-hand, borrowed from the teller's grand-parent or cousin. Some were recent incidents; others happened as long ago as the 1940s. In some of the stories, the identity of the ghost in question has been speculated about, with the storytellers expressing varying levels of conviction. In others, the sighting, and its afterlife as a tale to be spun, *is* the whole story, with no accompanying history to build a theory on. All the stories, however, have two things in common. First, they are incidents that took place in living memory: a specific manifestation, to a specific person, can be recalled. And, secondly, they've all clung on for months and often years in the memory of the witnesses, and the witnesses' witnesses – hauntings that repeat themselves whenever the mind, that most rest-less of spirits, wanders.

All of these stories are real, or certainly believed by the teller to be so. Some, like that of The House in Elspeth Street, are well-known in their community of origin: that ghost became an object of local curiosity, despite the alleged spirit not having been commonly sighted. Others, like the many and varied tales of Gibside's White Lady, are part of a collective record of multiple stories offering different outlooks on the same (assumed) ghost, often tessellating with local folklore to create little legends for children to whisper about.

The late Hilary Mantel once described ghosts as 'the tags and rags of everyday life, information you acquire that you don't know what to do with'. In telling each other ghost stories, we are peeling back not only the layers of our communities, but of ourselves; a tale that twists in the telling is not a lie, but *alive,* a haunting in progress.

So, come on: sit down. Close your eyes. *Whistle and I'll come to you.*

Let's tell some ghost stories.

Chapter One
House Guests

IN THE AUTUMN OF 2020, the Old Vic theatre in London lay empty and silent as a result of the coronavirus pandemic. Still, the show must go on, and in September, a three-actor cast performed Brian Friel's eerie *Faith Healer* with remarkable acuity and passion, given that their only audience – other than the invisible multitudes watching on Zoom – were the theatre's numerous ghosts. Early in Friel's play, the titular faith healer (a wild-haired, Pan-like Michael Sheen) explains that he and his psychic roadshow tour only in Wales and Scotland, the Celtic fringes where the borders are thin between our world and faeryland; where the people still believe.

As an exiled Geordie whose fascination with ghosts has had me mining and collecting for years the stories which now form the core of this book, it was clear to me that the troupe were missing a trick. Far from being something contained to vanishing pockets of our world, belief in the supernatural remains widespread and, in some of us, innate. Black Dogs, White Ladies, witches in the woods – we can find these stories everywhere. They are related around pub fireplaces, misremembered at teenage sleepovers. At Halloween and Hogmanay, a local legend or two is always fair game. These sorts of spectres are communal property, at once possessed by and possessing the people who believe in them.

The private ghost, however – the family ghost, or house guest – is a different thing entirely.

A considerable number of the first ghost stories I collected were family stories, in which otherwise unremarkable homes or streets played host to strange experiences shared in families, but little beyond. The private nature of the host locations – particularly where the homes were not frequently sold, nor in any other way forced to broadcast their eeriness – meant that the stories retained a private nature too. In some ways, I found these tales the most unsettling of all. However, I wasn't surprised by the number of private houses which, upon inquiry, gave up a ghost or two. To quote again the perennially perceptive Hilary Mantel, 'all houses are haunted' – including the one I grew up in, although I can't say I noticed at the time. Let's start there.

The Avenue

When my parents moved into the semi-detached house on the corner of The Avenue in Winlaton Mill, they had no thought of being frightened. On the contrary, they were sure this particular house would welcome them. My mother's grandparents, Kitty and George, had owned it from its construction in 1936 until George died and Kitty was persuaded, after much coaxing, to sell up and move into sheltered accommodation in nearby Winlaton. That was 1975. Twenty years later, my parents, now a young married couple with a three-year-old child, were in search of more room, only to find the house on the market once again. For Kitty's house to be available seemed like fate.

My mother was what was called 'indigenous' to the village: she had been born there, in a two-up two-down terraced house, and still seems to have every intention of dying there. In a village like this one, a shift from one street to another was about the boldest move that might be expected. My father, born five miles afield in neigh-bouring Newcastle, was an object of some curiosity for years after he moved in with his new wife. After all, the village didn't know him, and he didn't know it, with all its quirks and intricacies, its habits and its ghosts.

He would, however, soon come to.

The young couple quickly set to modernising Kitty's house which, while beautiful, was not selective in the original features it retained. Hand in hand with the deep bay windows went the single-glazing that had been installed there in 1936. Various strange alcoves had been built into clefts either side of the chimney breast which, itself, needed knocking out. Meanwhile, in the years between Kitty's reign and my mother's, the interim owner,

Denise, had put in a few monstrosities that had been the height of 1970s style and which were now ubiquitously accepted as eyesores. A set of built-in wardrobes, in particular, prompted shudders: Kitty would have been affronted by the mere idea.

I never met Kitty and George, but they were familiar to me from pictures tinted that slightly strange yellow colour so common to 1960s photography. George, a bus driver, was a transplant from Yorkshire and spoken of in the village as 'a foreigner' for the entire duration of his forty-year residence there. Tall and bald-headed, he looked charming, easy-going and deferential. Kitty, petite and glamorous, had been something of a beauty queen in her youth and acerbically referred to the 1970s as 'the decade that style forgot'. It was not difficult to imagine how she would have felt about the reconfiguring of her master bedroom in olive-tinted MDF.

The wardrobes went. New ones were installed in their place. Dad papered and plastered, drilled and sledge-hammered and, by the following year, the house had been transformed. The young family were very happy in it and, shortly afterwards, another baby was born: Elizabeth.

Unlike her older sister (I could never be induced to shut up), Elizabeth took her time learning to talk. She walked at nine months, but it wasn't until she was a year old that she said her first word. Once this milestone was passed, however, she seemed determined to make up for it. She chattered to her grandmother; to the milkman; to her dolls; to the television, as if imagining it could hear.

She began to talk to herself at night in her bedroom, laughing and babbling after the light had been extinguished. My mother thought little of it; after all, I at this age could often be found arranging glass beads in a circle and addressing them sombrely like the prime minister speaking to Parliament. When asked, Elizabeth said she was talking to 'The Man'. This seemed vague enough not to be a cause for concern.

As Elizabeth grew older, her bedtime conversations with The Man became increasingly eloquent and lengthy. Listening at the door, my mother observed that there was only ever one side to the conversation – Elizabeth never tried to fill in for her interlocutor. It was, she supposed, an imaginary friend. It didn't seem to be doing Elizabeth any harm, so she left it alone. Occasionally, Elizabeth would talk to The Man when Mam was in the room with her, which she liked rather less. One day, Elizabeth pointed out a television newsreader and expressed her delight that he was bald, 'like the man who lives in my room'.

Like any right-thinking young mother, Mam was more disturbed by this, but Elizabeth's room was only six feet by nine with a child's single bed. There was certainly nowhere for an uninvited visitor to hide. When my father returned from work and heard this development, he teased that he'd thought Elizabeth was developing a Yorkshire accent – 'Maybe she's talking to your grandad?' At my mother's blanch, he took her by the shoulders and smiled. 'Don't be silly. I'm kidding. She's picked that up from *The Chuckle Brothers*.'

'To me, to you,' Elizabeth volunteered obligingly from her position in front of the television, and Dad laughed.

'See? The Man will go away.'

He did. By the time Elizabeth was six, The Man was a thing of the past. When asked about him, she barely remembered.

One day, my mother bumped into the previous owner of her house, Denise, in the queue at the post office. In line with village expectation and tradition, she hadn't moved far when downsizing, and now occupied a small terrace in the next street. Denise was buying, among other things, Mint Imperials.

'Your grandad's favourite,' Denise said, seeing my mother looking. 'He was such a lovely man.'

Mam hesitated, and then joked: 'We certainly think Elizabeth likes him.'

Denise raised a quizzical eyebrow, and my mother explained about The Man. 'She was getting a sort of Yorkshire accent. We used to joke it was Grandad.'

Denise smiled. 'He's probably keeping her company while your granny does her routine with the curtains.'

My mother was puzzled by this, and said so.

'Doesn't she do your curtains for you?' Denise sounded unconcerned, amused. 'You must be better trained than I ever was. If I got up too late, there'd be the living room curtains open when I went downstairs. If I left it too late before I shut them, I'd go to the kitchen or something and come back and they'd be closed. Especially if the lights were on and I hadn't done it yet.'

'She couldn't abide that,' my mother admitted, remembering. 'Curtains, *then* lights.'

Denise paid for her Mint Imperials and waited while the postmistress scanned my mother's basket of bits and pieces. 'It never bothered us,' Denise said. 'It was just so Kitty. *I'll not have that kind of behaviour in my house.* I think she just wanted to give us a fright.'

That night, my mother stood deliberately in the broad bay window, curtains open, and turned on the overhead light. Of course, the curtains didn't so much as twitch. When she felt brave enough, she even tried walking into the kitchen and counting to a hundred before returning, just in case. But there was no rattle of curtain rings from the other room; no aggrieved veiling of the floodlit living room against prying eyes in the street.

'She likes what we've done with the place,' my father joked later. 'She was getting Denise back for those wardrobes.'

My mother laughed, too, but for her, Denise's information confirmed what she'd already believed: that Granny Kitty approved of them living in the house – new wardrobes, aspirational curtain etiquette and all.

The Man never appeared again. Two years later, when Elizabeth was eight and increasingly long of leg, the family accepted that a room barely wider than a single bed wouldn't suit her much longer. It was time to move.

Just before the exchange, the deeds to the house mysteriously vanished. My mother, having turned the place upside down in desperation, decided to try one final thing. She apologised to Kitty. 'Granny, I'm sorry we're going, but you know that room's not big enough for Elizabeth anymore. We've loved living here. We're not going far.'

When she searched again, dredging the same depths and turning over the same stones, she found the deeds, neatly folded beneath the box that held her rarely worn eternity ring. This was where they should have been in the first place. They had not, however, been there two hours earlier. Mam was dead certain of it – 'but of course,' she admitted, 'I could have been mistaken.'

There was no more trouble after that. The movers came, and there were no unplanned mishaps; nobody slipped on the stairs or inadvertently shattered any mirrors. So much had been made to fit the house that there was no point in taking it, so things like light fixtures and curtains remained, as did a custom-designed fireguard and, of course, the fitted wardrobes. It was midsummer and the new occupants wouldn't be taking possession for two days. Not wanting the house to become unbearably hot, my mother closed the bedroom curtains and thanked Kitty for her understanding.

'They're nice people,' she said. 'You'll like them. She's got great taste.'

It wasn't until we'd reached the end of the street – two adults, two children and a rabbit crammed into one small Mazda – that Mam looked back and saw that the bedroom curtains were open.

*

I was twelve years old when we moved, although the story of The Man and the mislaid deeds was kept from me until sometime later. My family believes in ghosts, but also in keeping them, sensibly, from children where possible. My stoic grandfather and his oldest son Lindsay, men of manual occupations and few words, both claimed to have seen the local White Lady on numerous occasions; Grandad had even seen a coach and horses. These sightings were shared without fanfare, but not until a child was too old to think a ghost could actually *hurt* you. Lindsay subsequently spent many years working in a power station whose various ghosts he often saw and heard, stalking the halls by night. His colleagues believed him. If Lindsay said there was a ghost, there was a ghost. He was that sort of man.

We weren't moving far. I spent the rest of my teenage years in the same short-vowelled, long-memoried community which first sparked my interest in ghosts – the sort of place which might serve as an avatar for many other, similar settlements, all with their own analogous hauntings. When I was a child, in the dim and distant days of the 1990s, a car journey of any length usually necessitated an hours-long wrestling match between the passenger and a map the size of a duvet. My mother, habitually cast in the role of passenger, had an even harder time than most, because our map didn't actually have Winlaton Mill marked on it. The surrounding villages were on there – Winlaton, Rowlands Gill, Blaydon – but not ours. The idea seemed to be that nobody would ever want to find the village if they didn't already know where it was, which gives some indication of the sort of place Winlaton Mill is.

The thing is, though, the map and its inadequacies didn't tell the full story. A map, like the uppermost layer of icing on an elaborate cake, shows us only the most recent incarnation of anything: the latest developments in the roadways and where one might, finally, be able to stop and address a child's urgently expressed need for the loo. To be fair to maps, that is generally what we turn to them for, albeit now it is more usually a swipe on a screen. Superficially, we look at a map to find out how to get somewhere. If we look closer, however, we can find much more. A map is not only a geographer's tool, but a historian's too. The topographical features and the abandoned monuments; the little roads that seem to stop in the middle of nowhere – that is where we find the layers underneath, the years of history underpinning the new motorway or the bypass which follows the route of an abandoned railway line. In the quiet, unlooked-for details of maps, we find the ghosts in whose afterlives we all now exist.

There's a painting which hangs, as if by royal decree, on the wall of every living room in the village. There was a copy in my grandmother's house, and one in ours. There was one in my uncle's back kitchen. (Winlaton Mill is very much the sort of place where everyone lives within two streets of their grandmother, and where people still have back kitchens. You know the sort of place. Perhaps your grandmother had a back kitchen, too.) I saw the painting so often that I can picture it in my mind line for line: a small cluster of houses by the bank of a narrow river, with a blue bridge in the foreground. The painting shows the Old Mill, which stood on the banks of the Derwent until the houses, though picturesque, were declared unfit for habitation and demolished in 1937. By this time, the new village, a series of red brick terraces and semis arranged in parallel lines, had been built on the opposite side of the road, and the residents moved. The road marks the bottom of a valley that slopes down from nearby Whickham; the village streets themselves are steep, inclining up towards the parish town of Winlaton. Because the village is, by British standards, new – no thatched cottages or dry-stone walls, just identical brick houses tucked into a cleared pocket of land surrounded by forest – it could easily be thought unremarkable, as our impertinent map seemed to suggest. Certainly not the sort of place that might appear in a horror film: young couple moves into Gothic dream house; dream house promptly devours them.

It's a favourite trick of museums to show the strata upon which a town is built. Here, perhaps many metres below current street level, is where the Romans built their road. A few feet above, archaeologists have uncovered shards of Tudor pottery. Above that, we find the effluvia of industry, the paved-over footprint of a town's lost expertise in steel or china or coal. We are all standing, at all times, on the ghosts of the past. Every town is built on the corpses of its previous incarnations.

The North-East, like much of Yorkshire, Wales and Cornwall, has been shaped by the pits that were sunk there, where the ore was mined out of the earth until there was nothing left. When the pits were closed, mining communities became, for a long time, 'former mining communities', defined by what they had lost. Winlaton Mill, in fact, was built on iron.

It's quite an odd story. A blacksmith's son rejoicing in the name of Ambrose Crowley III climbed the ranks of London society, Dick Whittington-style, to become sheriff, after which he was awarded a knighthood. The ironworks he established in the Derwent Valley in the latter years of the 1690s quickly became the biggest industrial centre in Europe. More fantastical still is the proto-communist empire Crowley established in nearby Winlaton, where his workers, known as Crowley's Crew, had an electoral committee, sick pay and guaranteed pensions in return for their loyalty (although, let's not forget, they were locked into their compounds at night).

Looking at it today, there is little indication that Winlaton Mill was ever a thriving seat of industry. Yet, when the Crowley Ironworks finally closed, they simply gave way to the next phase of the Mill's journey through great North-Eastern graft: the Derwenthaugh Cokeworks which opened in 1928, and steamed away until Thatcher closed them sixty years later. The slag, or by-product, of these cokeworks, soon overlaid the spot where the old village once stood. I remember, as a child, gazing out of the car window at the looming slag heaps that lay beside the road for years after the cokeworks shut down. In the 1990s, the site was reclaimed by the council and, as time went by, wildlife began to return to the area. The spindly little trees I remember being planted in protective jackets are now vast and verdant, lining the carriageway from Swalwell to Rowlands Gill. Four hundred years of heavy industry and hard slog have been swallowed up by Derwent Walk Country Park, as if they had never been.

My sister, five years younger than I am, has no memory of the slag heaps. In her mind, the village has always been what it is now: an unremarkable island of aspirational working-class houses, couched amid forestland like something out of Grimm's *Fairy Tales*. Even when a place's history is both representative and radical, it's easy enough for that to be covered up. All you need to do is lay some sod and plant some trees. Once the biggest ironworks in Europe; now too small to be shown on the map. *Plus ça change* – and yet the layers underneath are still there, the presence and the ringing absence of what once was. The same thing has happened all over the country, particularly in the sorts of areas often referred to as 'former'. *Former* fishing villages. *Post*-industrial towns. Every few years, the tall ships return to the Tyne like ghosts of the halcyon era when Newcastle's shipyards simply could not produce output quickly enough.

If an imprint as deep as Ambrose Crowley's on Winlaton Mill can be so thoroughly overlaid by time, it is a surety that other, similar villages all over the country will have forgotten wilder stories. The point is, what haunts places, and people, need not always be the madmen and the murderers; the iron magnates and the great ladies. As time marches inexorably on, we may cover up the marks we have made on the landscape with cokeworks which give way to country parks, but we do not eradicate them. They are still there, lying quiet, spirits dormant but not obliterated. From time to time, a flash of that buried spirit is unearthed, and its appearance in the modern world can be as *unheimlich* and unsettling as that of any ghost. A glimpse of the past quickens the heartbeat and shortens the breath, even an earthenware bottle found half-buried in the woods or a Victorian farthing. It is immaterial who once lost the farthing or drank from the bottle. The point is that we can hold these things in our hands, these artefacts of a past which, we now recognise, is not gone, but only hidden, and *imagine*. A ghost is just a different kind of ingression of the past into our present, a reminder of continuity which, however anonymous, thrills us in the same way.

The Figure on the Stairs

The Bottom Road separates the New Mill from the site of the Old Mill which, years ago, was superseded by the cokeworks and, subsequently, the Derwent Country Park. A slightly dissolute-looking garage stands between a very steep bank and a flight of even steeper steps which mark the two passable routes up into the village. (The third route, slightly further down the road, is Clockburn Lonnen, the road which once served 16,000 Roundhead soldiers but up which you could now barely fit a pushbike. A dilapidated sign at the top of it begs wearily for drivers to STOP, standing testament to the fact that, a few decades ago, it was traversable by cars. Another little ghost.)

In front of the garage stands a bus shelter which, at various points in time, has had windows on two sides, on one, and on none at all, at the mercy of local youth. On the other side of the road, a public house marks the only other sign of non-automotive life within eyeshot to anybody waiting at the shelter. Today called The Red Kite, it once served the Old Mill, which makes sense of its position, now rather isolated.

When Amy got off a bus home from Newcastle alone one night in 2004, The Red Kite's quiet presence did little to make her feel any less alone in the dark. She was nineteen. Anybody who has ever been a nineteen-year-old girl can bear witness to the fact that, at that age, while the fear of darkness itself may have been long since consigned to childhood, the fear of what might be lurking in it is just beginning to solidify. When Amy thanked the driver and stepped out onto the side of the road, the awareness of her own vulnerability seemed to weigh in on her from all sides. It wasn't that the village was rife (as my grandmother would say) with crime, but it *was* dark, and quiet, and Amy's house was still a fair walk away.

She considered the two possible routes home. Neither was particularly appealing. The climb up the bank was at exactly the worst possible gradient for the calves and thighs, and the stairs felt as if they hadn't been cut quite right, forcing an uneven, hopping gait upon any ascender. Still, the stairs were closer, and the journey up them – while steep and uncomfortable – tended to be faster. Amy set her jaw, shrugging off the unease that trickled down her spine, and turned in that direction.

Her foot was on the bottom-most step when she saw the man. He had not, she was sure, been there a moment before, when she'd assessed the shadowy staircase from the bus stop, fifty yards away. Walled on either side, the staircase comprised perhaps a hundred steps. About halfway up was a lamppost, the old-fashioned kind, like the sort that sprung up from a fragment in Narnia. If the council had known it was there, they would probably have come to replace it, but for now it remained, the lamp itself quirked at a slight angle, bathing the steps in its orange sodium light. Beneath it stood the unanticipated figure.

God, Amy thought to herself, heart sinking. *A man.*

It was a winter evening, and the man was in a hat and overcoat, his face in shadow. At this distance, she struggled to gauge his age or ethnicity, but she could see that he was slight – even frail. She decided to take her chances.

She cast her eyes downward as she began her uncomfortable ascent. Two steps across each poorly engineered stair, and then another step up. Her breath was coming faster, and the stationary figure of the man was getting closer. She glanced up at intervals, eyeing him warily. Dreading the moment their paths must necessarily cross.

Except that, when she reached the stair below his – when she looked up into the pool of orange light cast by the lamppost onto the central stair – the man was gone. It was difficult to parse the feeling that welled up in her chest. Her eyes cut from side to side; from one six-foot wall to the other. There was no way the man could have vaulted out of the confines of the stairwell without her noticing. There was no way he could have sprinted up to the street above in the seconds since she'd last passed her eyes warily over him. It was not humanly possible, a thought which clutched coldly at the base of her spine. But, on the other hand, she was no longer alone in a dark stairwell with a potential assailant.

Amy took a breath, took courage from the sliver of relief this thought occasioned, and ran. She took the steps two at a time to the deserted street at the top, then hurtled along, gasping, to the corner, where her parents lived. Amy did not, as a rule, run; indeed Amy had made it almost a personality trait never to move faster than necessary, so when she arrived at her front door still panting with effort, her mother was understandably concerned.

'Amy?' White-faced with alarm, the woman ushered her daughter inside. 'What's wrong – *Amy?*'

Amy took a moment, doubled over, to come back to herself. The memory of the man on the steps was strong, but stronger still was the thought of the relief when she'd seen he'd disappeared.

'I've seen a ghost,' she said, breathless. Her mother's eyebrows shot up into her hairline.

'Are you all right?' She gripped her daughter by both arms, unnerved. 'Petal?'

'I'm all right,' Amy assured her, trying to smile. 'I was more scared when I thought it was a man.'

Her mother, still startled, managed to smile back. She pulled Amy into her arms. 'Better a dead man in the dark than a live one.'

*

Amy tells her story unapologetically, with a shrug. She has no suggestions as to who the figure might have been; she is, however, entirely convinced that no living man could have vanished so precipitately, between one blink and the next. Perhaps someone, she suggests, from a time before the walls were built? But, she explains, 'it doesn't matter. I'm glad I saw him, because I was more frightened *before* he disappeared. Him being a ghost wasn't so bad.' For Amy, her sole spectral sighting proved fortifying – proof of the fact that the paranormal is not the most terrifying thing one could encounter. It isn't the dead . . . usually . . . who pose a threat.

As she ran home in the dark that night, Amy would have passed the house where Tom and his parents lived. The two didn't know each other: Tom is five years younger than Amy and went to a different primary school.

For Amy, her brief encounter with the man on the stairs marked a lone instance of divergence from a life otherwise untroubled by the intrusion of the supernatural. For Tom, it was a different story.

Ken

Somebody in the Laughlan house, Tom told me, is looking for Ken. Tom, now twenty-six, lived in the house from the age of eight until he left to start his own family at twenty-three. His parents and two sisters live there still, and all of them are in accord that at least one unregistered occupant keeps them company. Ken, Tom thinks, is not among the spectral subletters. That seems to be the root of the problem.

With three children in a three-bedroomed house, there was inevitably some argument over rooms. The master bedroom was for Mam and Dad; Tom, the middle child, slept in the second bedroom with his younger sister until, when he was ten, a ceremonial exchange was conducted. The seniority of his older sister Jasmine had to buckle to the need for sex segregation, which meant Tom, the lone boy, would now be in his own room for the first time ever, falling asleep unaccompanied by the sound of someone else's breathing.

That was the plan, anyway.

It was almost soothing, to lie in the dark and listen to another person's gentle sleep-sounds – and the rhythm of his sister's breathing had so long been a part of Tom's bedtime routine that at first he didn't even recognise the new sound as anomalous. It wasn't until he heard the woman's voice in his ear – 'Ken? Ken!' – that he realised it wasn't his sister he could hear.

He'd dreamed it, he told himself, and tried to settle. He was a big boy now, after all; he couldn't embarrass himself by running to his mother. The thing was that, if it was a dream, it was certainly a persistent one. Tom heard the voice, saying Ken's name, almost every night for weeks.

One morning, he and Jasmine were in their parents' bedroom folding washing, the sunlight streaming through the open window, when a sudden clatter and a shout from the landing stopped them mid-motion. An unfamiliar woman's voice echoed in the stairwell: 'Ken?' The next second, the family cat shot into the room like a fat and frightened bullet, her tail brush-stiff and upright, quivering.

The siblings looked at each other in alarm, but Tom thought there was something else, too, in the expression on Jasmine's face. After they'd checked the (of course, empty) landing for signs of life, Jasmine asked, 'Have you heard her before?'

Tom nodded, awash with relief.

'Mam said I wasn't allowed to tell you,' Jasmine said, 'in case you got scared. She never *does* anything.'

'She's just looking for Ken,' Tom agreed.

They heard the woman in daylight after that, from time to time: a sigh on the stairs, or a slightly rueful 'Ken, Ken, *Ken*' uttered out of nothingness in the living room. Once, when the three siblings – now teenagers – were gathered on the sofa engaged in a lively argument over the PlayStation controller, all three looked up to meet the eyes of a little girl peering through the glass panel of the door – as if, Tom said, she'd like to have a turn, too. Still no sign of Ken.

The little girl was never glimpsed again after that encounter, but the Laughlans posit that she, too, was probably on the hunt for him. Sometimes, at night, Tom recalls the coal-dark eyes in the little white face and thinks, whoever she was, he hopes she's found Ken.

Actually, Ken's whereabouts are readily identifiable. The Laughlans bought the house from a widow, Marion. When consulting the deeds and the floorplan prior to building an extension, Mrs Laughlan spotted the name of Marion's husband among the papers: Ken. At rest in the local church-yard beneath an ostentatious stone, Ken's presence has never made itself known in the house since he left it; the Laughlans have never heard a masculine voice among the whispers.

The mysterious woman and child are another matter. Tom has tried to persuade the lady. 'I've told her: Ken's not here. He's dead. But she didn't take any notice. It's as if she can't hear.'

'They don't bother us so much, after all this time,' Jasmine added. 'They're not interested in us. They're just looking for Ken.'

*

In the early stages of working on this book, I told the story of the Laughlans' house to a colleague. The voice, with its repeated phrases, was interesting, I said. The colleague laughed rather humourlessly, and said, 'It happens more often than you think. At least they know it's only Ken she wants.'

The colleague was male, middle-aged, and pragmatic. He had grown up in the Home Counties and looked rather sheepish about having said anything at all, but: horse, stable door, bolt. I pushed, of course. He told me.

'Come Here'

George's parents separated when he was thirteen, a particularly difficult age for a child to have to confront such a seismic change. The pleasant family house was sold; George's father moved into a flat, while he and his mother shifted three streets away into a rented ex-council property, a fixer-upper with smart period features buried beneath layers of mid-century 'improvements'.

'Come on,' his mother said, 'we've got to make the best of it. It's a nice house.'

George, disconsolate but not wishing to make things more difficult than they needed to be, made a grudging promise to *try* to like the house. It was, after all, a stone's throw from their last one; he wouldn't have to change schools or abandon his friends. They could make the house their own. It had good bones.

That's what they say, isn't it? *Good bones.* He'd never liked the phrase.

For a week or two, things were tolerable. The house creaked at night as all houses do, but George's mother had a ready explanation: it was 'settling'. Now it was up to her and George to settle, too.

George's mum was a cleaner who was rarely there when he let himself into the house after school. When, after a fortnight in the house, George opened the door to the smell of cooking, his heart leaped hopefully. She must have come home early, he thought, to surprise him. He deposited his schoolbag in the hall and called out, 'Mum?'

'Come here,' said a female voice.

George bristled. The voice was strident, cross, as if George had done something wrong. Indignant, he stalked towards the kitchen, ready to defend himself if necessary. Whatever she'd heard, it was a lie! George had been good as gold at school! He thrust open the door belligerently, poised to make his case to his mother.

The kitchen was completely, definitively, empty. On the far side of the room, however, the oven light was on, a frill of grey smoke just beginning to emerge from around the door. Suddenly cold with horror, it took George some moments to gather the presence of mind to cross the room and turn it off.

He left the room as quickly as he'd entered it. Catching his breath in the living room, his mind raced through possible explanations. These were terraced houses, the dividing walls barely two bricks thick. Sometimes acoustics were strange – the sound of someone else's mother manifesting in the wrong stairwell, filtering out of one kitchen window and in through another. George tried to calm his racing heart and be rational. He didn't know this house yet. They were unacquainted. *Settling.*

Gingerly, he sat down on the edge of the sofa, head between his knees as his games teacher had taught him. The house still smelled smoky, the scorched aftermath of other people's baked-on grime. The dizziness was receding, but the back of George's neck felt exposed, prickling.

Suddenly, from somewhere a metre or so to the right of him, George heard the voice again: 'George. Come *here.*'

George raced out of the house with his eyes averted, keys abandoned, the front door banging behind him.

When his mother came home an hour later, she found George perched on the garden wall, still vaguely trembling. For some reason, when George opened his mouth to explain about the voice, he found he couldn't do it. Instead he said, 'The oven turned itself on, Mum.'

'What?' Alarmed, George's mother sped into the house to investigate. She inspected the dials, the settings, the timer. Eventually, unable to find any issue, she turned the oven off at the wall.

'There,' she said. 'Whatever's wrong, that'll sort it for now.'

George slept tensely, nervously all that night. When he got home from school the following day, the house was filled with smoke. He had to force himself to hurtle through it like a soldier through chlorine gas, lingering just long enough to turn off the oven at the wall – again. Something, or someone, had flipped the switch. George didn't care to stay long enough to discover who.

It was a process, of course. George's mother's first thought was that George was, as she put it, 'creating', although it seemed very out of character. Only when they came home together one Saturday to the same unsettling sight did she call an electrician, who also could find nothing wrong. After that it was time to escalate the problem to the landlord.

Another week or two passed, and she decided they should cut their losses. 'This house is going to burn down at this rate,' she said. 'I don't want us to be here when it does.'

A year later, George says, it did. The landlord blamed faulty wiring, but George isn't so sure.

'Sometimes I think *something* did it,' he admits, 'and whatever it was knew my name.' He hesitates. 'I'm being silly.'

(He doesn't really think this. He just doesn't want to look too squarely at the other possibility.)

*

In some parts of the United States, there is a legal obligation to disclose if a person has ever died in a house. To those of us in the United Kingdom, this seems a provision that could only be expected in a youthful country: between 2015 and 2018, I lived in an Oxfordshire house that had nurtured generations of families since before the United States of America existed as a nation. I wouldn't be shocked to discover that numerous people had been born and died there. In fact, I'd be astonished if they hadn't.

Houses are strange things – old houses, even more so. I don't mean simply houses that have existed for a long time, but houses that belong to the older parts of ourselves, the places we once knew well enough to navigate our way to the loo in the dark, and which we have no real expectation of ever seeing again. In our 'haunted house' my mother marked my changing heights on the dining room door frame. Those marks will have been painted over now, long since rendered invisible, but the other, subtler marks we make on our homes can't be so easily eradicated. We fill them up with our joy and our pain; houses cast shadows, bear scars and leave them. Perhaps the ghosts in your house don't whisper in the night like the unknown woman searching for Ken, but that doesn't mean they don't exist.

The vast majority of the family ghost stories I heard revolved around what were presumed to be once-human visitors. This was, however, not always the case. In York, I was told a story which diverged slightly from the rest. Lest we forget, there's more to many families than their human members. Animals live and die with us, too, in our houses and, in many cases, in our legends.

Jet

Sarah first saw Jet from the window the day her father came home from hospital to die.

She'd never been allowed a dog. Her mother said, not unreasonably, that their narrow three-bed terrace in central York wasn't the place for an animal, an argument Sarah understood, but still couldn't quite accept. Like many Victorian houses in the area near the train station – now being slowly gentrified – there wasn't so much a garden as a high-walled yard, opening onto a ginnel in which generations of children once played. An enterprising cat might be able to pick its way in, via the roof of the disused coalhouse, and sun itself on the flagstones. A dog would need to have developed the power of flight. Nevertheless, there Jet was.

This was April of 1974. As her father's pancreatic cancer worsened, Sarah, then fifteen, had spent much of her time with her bedroom door closed, playing Wings' *Band on the Run* until the needle began to wear a groove in the record. The album was the sound of that spring in general, but for Sarah, it resonated: *Jet, I thought the only lonely place was on the moon . . .*

The dog, something between a black Labrador and a shaggy Newfoundland, was instantly Jet in Sarah's mind. There was, she said, nothing spectral about it. It did not have red eyes or cloven hooves. It didn't snarl or howl. It simply sat there patiently, a large black dog in a place where a dog could not possibly be.

The master bedroom, where Sarah's father had been lovingly settled into bed, looked the opposite way, onto the steep front street with its established trees. Only Sarah's window overlooked the yard. From it, she could see Jet clearly; when she called to him, he raised his eyes obediently to her. When she ventured downstairs, filing through the galley kitchen to the back door, the yard was empty. No dog.

A stray, Sarah told herself, but a shiver picked its way across her shoulders. What sort of stray could vault a wall taller than a man, then reprise the feat in reverse, in silence?

Jet continued to appear over the weeks that followed. Sarah, under the most unforgiving of circumstances, was revising for nine O-levels. The dog was an odd sort of comfort to her: she would lift her head from her books and glance out of the window to see him there, upright on the flagstones, stalwart.

Waiting for Dad, Sarah thought. For some reason, she was utterly and gratefully convinced that Jet was waiting for Dad – not as a looming threat, but as a companion who would escort him home when the time came.

Dad, meanwhile, seemed to be waiting for Sarah. He outlasted the doctors' predictions, clinging on through the melee of exam season. Every morning, Sarah would go in to be kissed and wished good luck. Not *every* afternoon – but often enough – she would return to her bedroom to glimpse Jet from the window, sitting closer now. Everything was closer now.

Sarah's father died in August, slightly too early to hear that she had passed her nine O-levels successfully, despite it all. After that, she never saw the dog again. His wait was over.

*

What interested me most about Sarah's story was her interpretation of the Jet apparition. The Black Dog is one of the most recognised motifs in all of British folklore: from the churchyard Grim, popularised by J. K. Rowling in her Harry Potter novels, to the Welsh *Gwyllgi* and the Devon Yeth Hound, the dog is usually understood to be an omen of death. Often described as 'hellhounds', these beasts typically come with all the supernatural trappings of a demonic entity, from red eyes to clanking chains. Normally, such entities are considered manifestations of the Devil. To interact with a Black Dog usually occasions death. A Black Dog is also often a metaphor for depression, a heavy dark presence that stalks you against your will.

Jet was something else. In northern English folklore, the Black Dog is called 'Barghest', a term thought to derive from 'burh-ghest', or 'town ghost'. It's also mooted that it may derive from German 'Bahr-Geist', the spirit of the funeral bier. The connection between the dog and a coming death remains strong; however, the Barghest has its own local nuance. While its appearance predicts that a death is to come, there is rarely an indication that it *causes* death. A Barghest might lie across the threshold of a person's house as an indication that their death is imminent. It is also said to have the capacity to incite all the living dogs of the area into a sort of mournful Twilight Bark to herald the passing of a significant person. While there is no account that I could find of a Barghest taking on the psychopomp role Sarah ascribed to Jet – a spirit whose role it is to escort deceased souls to the afterlife – it is undeniable that the Barghest is perhaps the gentlest of the Black Dog archetypes.

The Barghest, incidentally, is strongly associated with northern towns such as Sunderland, Whitby and York. Indeed, one of the houses in York's famous crooked street, The Shambles, is called *Barghest*. Perhaps the idea was on Sarah's mind. Anyone who has ever played Chinese Whispers will know how tales change with the telling. Is it possible that demonic entities can be reshaped by shifting, or even misinformed, beliefs? Does the Barghest, like any stray dog, only need a little love?

It's certainly a question.

*

Jet isn't the only animal spirit I've encountered on my travels through other people's pasts. For some, the question of whether or not animals have souls is a philosophical dilemma to be wrestled with, but for many pet owners, the answer is straightforward. It's difficult to live with an animal for years, watching its little thoughts flicker across its little face, and feel you haven't seen its soul. Jet is unusual in that he did not have his origins in a physical pet of Sarah's, but the conviction that our canine and feline companions return to us after their deaths is one held by many.

I came across numerous brief and very similar accounts of pet hauntings – seemingly the most desired, benign and comforting of all. Many people are also especially ready to share these stories unabashedly, as if an animal ghost is less unhinged a thing in which to believe wholeheartedly.

Certainly, they appear to be less complicated. Our pets live to love us; they are only a part of our lives, but we are the whole of theirs. Why should this change just because their bodies have given up on them? Here are three of the cases that moved me most:

Daisy: Our ginger tabby, Archie, went missing one night. We were beside ourselves. He'd been gone three days when my husband came home, shouted his name, and then came pelting up the stairs to ask me when Archie had come back.

I asked him what he was talking about. He said, 'Archie's downstairs in his bed!'

We didn't have a cat flap – we let him in and out ourselves, at his beck and call whenever he wanted it. I hadn't let him in, but I wanted to think he'd come in somehow on his own, through a window or something. We both went back downstairs and he wasn't there.

An hour later, a vet rang to say his body had been handed in and they'd identified him by his chip. He'd been hit by a car. We were devastated. Then, that night in bed, I felt the mattress dip – the weight of a cat leaping onto it and then walking up my body. I put out my hand automatically to touch Archie, but there was nothing there. I knew he was, though.

Andrea: I had a shih-tzu called Sally who had to be put to sleep. I felt her get onto my bed for weeks afterwards, in the middle of the night, and sometimes I'd hear her snuffle. It stopped eventually and I missed it, but it was as if she wanted a transition period.

Paul: I see my tortoiseshell cat out of the corner of my eye quite often. She's been dead for about four years. Just after it happened, I used to feel her jump onto the bed with me. Once I woke in the night and she was on my pillow; I could feel her fur.

*

As I researched this book, I mentally categorised the sorts of ghosts I've described in this chapter – the plaintive voice on the landing of Tom's house; the unseen hand that twitched the curtains in The Avenue – as house guests. In reality, the term is so unimaginative as to be almost redundant. *Ghost*, after all, comes from Old English *gast*, or spirit; the same Indo-European root, a little further up the language tree, gives us *guest*. We can see the similarity, too, in modern German words like *zeitgeist*: the spirit, or ghost, of the times. The ghost and the guest are both spirits among us, separated only by the question of whether or not they have brought a corporeal form to stay.

What differentiates 'house guests', in my mind, from other types of haunting is their singularity, their private nature. Who knows how many similar spirits are lurking behind closed doors, in the locked hoards of family legend? In a place where belief in ghosts hovers close to the surface, the number might be higher than it is elsewhere, but one thing's for sure: any home in the country could be, at any time, harbouring an unexpected guest. It's an uncanny consideration, that there may be hidden threats, as well as private comforts, in our homes. We like to think of our communities as contained, impenetrable. It's disconcerting to discover that they aren't.

*

The family ghost, or house guest, is very much part of the fabric of life in a small community, but it is a different beast from the spirit which *belongs* to a community and, in some ways, defines it. Some of the *gasts* among us are not contained by four walls, or by individual memories. They walk not down the landings of semi-detached family homes, but through communities, often for generations, shaped by and reshaping their own histories.

In the village in which I grew up – as in hundreds upon thousands of small communities in Britain, Europe, and beyond – a White Lady walks. Reams of stories were reported to me about the White Lady of Gibside Hall, the Derwent Valley's most notorious spectral inhabitant. Some of them were rooted in the lurid history of her supposed living antecedent, Mary Eleanor Bowes. Some were deeply intertwined with topographical, social and historical elements of the local area, and could not have occurred anywhere else. Some, however, were more than a little familiar to me. Not every White Lady is Mary Eleanor Bowes, but from Winlaton Mill to Windsor Castle, Marrakech to Mexico, they all seem to have some things in common.

What exactly, then, is this creature, the White Lady? I was curious to discover why she was so pervasive in our cultural fabric, and how her lingering influence is felt in the communities that host her, but this seemed to invite a broader question. What is it about our White Ladies that makes them resonate with us down the centuries, with so many points of similarity in communities which otherwise seem radically disparate?

Let's find out.

Chapter Two
White Ladies

IN 2021, MY FRIEND and I inadvertently founded a literary journal. This is the sort of natural disaster which occurs when an unpredictable two years are spent pinballing between online teaching, MS Teams meetings and, perhaps worst of all, the tyranny of the Friday evening family Zoom chat. The journal, *The Banshee,* was (and is) subtitled 'the leading journal for women who scream' – with the caveat that it is, to our knowledge, the only such journal. A publication for supernatural yellers, emphatic prophets of doom, and those who scream inside their hearts, the first issue of *The Banshee* invited 'screams of laughter; screams of rage, fear, and delight'.

Perhaps the most surprising thing, given that this began life as a Twitter joke, was that we received numerous submissions, ran a successful Kickstarter campaign and so were able to embody screams from all around the world in A5 perfect-bound form. The second most surprising thing to me, however, was the motif that ran through so much of what we received: the creature which, for twenty-first-century women the world over, seemed to represent their frustrations, their fears, and the screams they could not otherwise release: *La Llorona*. The weeping woman; the White Lady.

Submission after submission took this archetype and repurposed or reinvented it, particularly intriguing because the titular banshee – the crying spirit of Irish folklore, a harbinger of death – made no appearances whatsoever in our inbox. In some ways, this seems odd. The ghost stories a society tells itself are a way of holding up a mirror to changing struggles, in the hope of identifying the loose end of the thread which might help us unravel our knots. Zombie dystopias represent a fear of plague, corruption and, sometimes, climate-based devastation. Horror films based around the loss of one or several senses, such as *Bird Box* or *A Quiet Place* (both 2018), seem to reflect a terror that we cannot trust the evidence of our eyes, nor safely speak our minds. What better figure, then, than the banshee, *bean chaointe*, whose wails presage the death of a family member, to help us make sense of a respiratory pandemic which has claimed the lives of hundreds of thousands?

Perhaps it's simply too hard to identify with a banshee, a she-faerie not of this world, who alerts us to the coming of pain she cannot herself understand. Nobody, after all, wants to be a harbinger of doom.

The banshee is not a uniquely Irish phenomenon. Although most commonly found in Irish mythology, her Gaelic lament has historically also been heard in parts of Scotland: the Rossmore banshee supposedly heralded a death in the family of Baron Rossmore. The Welsh *cyhyraeth*, a moaning spirit supposedly heard before a shipwreck around the River Tywi and on the Glamorganshire coast, represents a similar concept. In both cases, the manifestations typically occur dressed in white, and in connection with water, two elements also found in many White Lady stories.

However, neither the banshee or the *cyhyraeth* is typically a *lady*. These are supernatural creatures of the fairy otherworld; they have never lived. While occasionally they appear as beautiful virgins, they more commonly take the form of crones, their gnarled visages a representation of their great age and wisdom: these spirits know what we do not. The *cyhyraeth* is often believed to be a descendant form of a water spirit, a lingering cultural echo of Welsh mythology. The haunting sound of her voice on the wind at sea represents the fears of a seafaring people whose pagan beliefs have not yet fully died. But these creatures, while they both remain recognised figures of folklore, do not seem to have passed into the modern day in the same way as their analogue, the White Lady. My twenty-first century screamers saw in *La Llorona*, Dama Branca and Witte Wieven avatars for their own grief and frustration, figures with whom they resonated. But while these fiction-alised and analytical accounts of White Ladies show how deeply the archetype haunts our culture, her real-life hauntings also continue. White Ladies, I have found, are here to stay.

*

When I was a child, 'looking for the White Lady' was a common pursuit. On long summer evenings, we would cycle for miles with the hair prickling on the backs of our necks, anticipating her appearance. As we cycled, we were looking for a flash of white glimpsed from the corner of the eye, or another child barrelling back down the hill full pelt, looking as if he might (just might) have seen a ghost. We were looking to be frightened. This is the impulse that drives avid ghost hunters to track the remarkably peripatetic ghost of Anne Boleyn from Hever Castle to Blickling Hall to the Tower of London. It's the reason tourists linger in Marazion, hoping to catch a glimpse of a ghostly stagecoach transporting the White Lady to St Michael's Mount. But it doesn't explain the similarities between all these pallid women – nor the subtle differences in the stories we tell about them, varying not only with geographic distance, but with chronological distance too. It doesn't explain what drives us, all over the British Isles and beyond, to anticipate the same group of traits in a fly-by-night spectre defined by her gender. White Ladies, of course, are far from the only supernatural entity for whom this is true. What is it, then, that differentiates these beings in our minds?

What makes a female spirit a White Lady instead of another kind of ghost – or a witch?

The Unhappy Countess

Mary Eleanor Bowes of Gibside Hall led a colourful, stranger-than-fiction life. At one point the wealthiest heiress in Britain, the death in 1776 of her first husband, the Earl of Strathmore, ushered in a period of mounting excess and increasing disrepute for the Countess. An affair with the working-class George Gray resulted in multiple pregnancies, all of which were illegally aborted by Mary Eleanor while the affair continued. At this point in her life, Mary Eleanor was held in contempt by much of polite society, so it is interesting to find no trace of this in any of the White Lady stories that circulate about Gibside Hall. The vast majority revolve instead around her second marriage to Andrew Robinson Stoney, during which she gained the appellation of 'the Unhappy Countess'.

Stoney, an Anglo-Irish lieutenant posing as a captain in the British Army, was the man whose name gave rise to the phrase 'stoney broke', so persistent was his state of financial ruin. The story of his seduction of Mary Eleanor reads more like a tale of online sock puppet fraud than of eighteenth-century courtship. Intrigued by her vast wealth, he hit upon the idea of writing a series of articles for *The Morning Post,* under a false name, critiquing the countess's moral character. He also countered each article with a piece in her defence, and finally challenged the paper's editor to a duel for Mary's honour. Mary, romantic by nature, had no reason not to believe him when he claimed to be mortally wounded, and indulged his dying wish by marrying him. Nobody could have foreseen his sudden and miraculous recovery.

Despite the remarkable deviousness of this scheme, it seems that Mary, all too aware of the draw of her huge fortune, had nevertheless made a prenuptial agreement before meeting Stoney at the altar. In line with the wishes of Mary's now long-deceased father, he had taken her name: he meant to take her fortune too. By physical force, Stoney induced Mary to sign a revocation of the prenup, which had been intended to prevent him from controlling her wealth. Thus began a period of intense, sustained physical and mental abuse, during which Mary was frequently confined to Gibside Hall. In 1785, Mary staged a daring escape and filed for divorce on the grounds of cruelty. Stoney, unwilling to admit defeat, proceeded to abduct her.

Although there was initially much sympathy for Mary's plight at the time of her eventual rescue, the mores of the era placed heavy judgement upon her, both for her previous extramarital affairs and because of yet another entanglement with a lawyer which supposedly ensued during the ongoing divorce trials. Mary lost her battle against 1780s' public opinion; in 1800, she lost her life to an unrecorded illness at the age of fifty-one – some reports have it that she was buried in a pearl-studded bridal gown, as if hoping for a final, happy marriage in Heaven. But Stoney, too, lost his own battle to retain control of the

Bowes fortune, and later to invalidate Mary's will. He died, as he lived, in penury.

Mary lived her final years at Stourfield House in Hampshire, accompanied by her two daughters, her maid-servant, and an array of dogs upon whom she doted. The locals thought of her as an eccentric, but Mary found her own peace, pursuing a long-held interest in botany and devoting herself to her canine court until her frail health deteriorated – no doubt hastened by the abuse she had suffered. The once-grand Gibside Hall tumbled down over the following centuries. As any local will tell you, though, the grounds are still there, and the woods, and the parkland – and the dogged, determined White Lady.

The Orangery Dance

The evening was warm and, as Sergeant Robert Dodds made his way up the tree-lined path towards Gibside Hall in the summer of 1942, he could almost forget he had ever been away. France, with its bombs and its beaches, seemed like another world. Tonight, Robert was on leave and, like every other soldier, sailor and airman in the area, was on his way to Gibside's ornate orangery for a dance.

Dances at Gibside had once been a staple of Robert's Friday evenings; the orangery no longer had its roof, but it retained its charms. Previously, estate workers had festooned it in flowers, adorning the stone arches with drapery and lights. Now, flags took the place of the flowers, and every dance went ahead on the understanding that a cry of 'Lights out!' would send the whole place plunging into darkness. Only the night before had found Robert in the Anderson shelter with his mother and sisters, the four of them huddled together while bombers whirred overhead.

Still, Robert was excited. This was his first leave in months, and beyond the dance itself, he had something else to look forward to. Mabel had promised she'd be there.

Mabel. Robert quickened his pace at the mere memory of her green eyes, her dark hair. They weren't engaged – she teased that she planned to marry a sailor – but Robert had high hopes. He had known Mabel since she was twelve years old, and adored her for almost as long. Yes: a night couldn't help but be perfect if Mabel was part of it.

When he reached the orangery, dusk was just beginning to fall. There were some familiar faces: Ann, who'd been at school with him; Alastair Carter, a coal miner, whose occupation prohibited him from joining up. Alastair resented this, and Robert understood why – although he'd never sing the praises of soldiering, there were those at a dance like this who'd turn up their noses at a man like Alastair. *Soldiers Only.* Robert made sympathetic noises in Alastair's direction as the first of several girls coaxed him onto the dancefloor.

At first, Mabel's absence didn't trouble him. Mabel was a munitions worker, which meant long hours and hard graft, even before the twenty-minute bus journey from Newcastle. It wasn't until it was almost dark that Robert began to worry – to think that Mabel wasn't coming.

He couldn't think she'd stand him up, not after the way she'd sounded on the phone. She'd assured him she'd been looking forward to it. He knew her well enough for that. With each dance that followed, Robert paid less and less attention to his partner, and more to his surroundings, scanning the archways and angles of the orangery for the familiar face.

When he saw her, his heart clenched with relief. It was close to ten, far too late to *arrive* at a dance, but it was her, all right, a familiar figure in a white tea-dress, her hair loose around her face. In the low light of the lanterns, she looked more beautiful than ever, propped in the curve of an archway. Her eyes met his, and he smiled in gratitude.

The girl in his arms seemed to sense his inattention, looking up at him inquisitively. He felt a cad, but said, 'Margaret, please excuse me – I've just seen a friend.'

Margaret was disgruntled, predictably so, but Robert couldn't stand to waste too long consoling her. He apologised, then disentangled himself, looking up again towards the archway.

No Mabel. His spirits sank. She'd been there – he'd seen her! He took a step across the orangery, and then another, until he was standing where she had stood. A faint smell of orange blossom lingered in the air, like the memory of a girl's perfume.

For a moment he was nonplussed. Then, looking out of the warmly lit orangery and down into the valley below, he saw a figure in a white dress. Heartened, he hastened towards it. Mabel's name leaped from his lips.

The woman turned. Her long dark hair, he saw in an instant, was not Mabel's, with its deftly coiffed victory rolls. Her long white dress was not the fashionable tea-dress Mabel had worn. The look on her face, though, carried something of Mabel in it: something soft and sympathetic and sad. That look stole the breath from Robert's lungs, even before the woman – gently, gradually, almost apologetically – disappeared into the darkness.

Robert stood in silence for a long moment. Of course, he knew about Gibside's White Lady. As a child, he even fancied he'd seen her once, a pale flicker glimpsed out of the corner of an eye. But he'd never thought to see her like this, so soft and clear in her regard of him. He'd imagined her as detached, filmy, perhaps something like a recording, observed in her final flight – not as this vividly realised young woman who had looked directly at him with such intent. She'd looked, he would later say, as if she'd come to comfort him, in fulfilment of a promise not her own.

Some minutes later, Robert made his way back up to the half-ruined orangery, where the dance was still ongoing. Ann, detaching herself from the grasp of a half-cut sailor, moved over to him, touched his arm.

'Margaret says you were calling for Mabel,' she said gently.

'I thought I'd seen her,' Robert explained. 'In the archway.'

Ann's face twisted. The look of sympathy upon it was so familiar that Robert felt instantly sick. Even before she spoke, he knew what she was going to say.

'The night before last,' she ventured. 'The air raid. Didn't you know?'

Afterwards, Robert would relate this incident and say that he never believed it had been Mabel who had come to the orangery that day. Mabel, in fact, had been dead two days, and was even then lying in a Newcastle morgue. Somebody else, however, had come in her stead, unwilling to leave him waiting at the dance. The White Lady of Gibside was not the woman Robert waited for, but that night, at least, she was the one who was there.

*

The story of the soldier in the orangery is only one of many Gibside Hall White Lady stories. I chose to include it here because of what it indicates about how stories can change in the telling – how they can collect new ghosts along the way. In this case, the ghost is not only the Lady herself, but also the spirit of the recent past: the war which shaped this community as much as it did most and lingers in the collective memory. For the local spirit to become embedded into that mesmeric setting seems a beautifully natural outcome.

To be embedded in a setting is one thing, but this White Lady is certainly no longer confined to one. Her roaming grounds are vast, and while those who set out to pin her down in obvious places are often disappointed, ramblers further afield have seen the spectre completely unexpectedly – especially in the twilight hours, as frequent rambler Charlotte discovered.

Charlotte's story is only one variation on a very common theme; numerous people reported similar sightings, white flashes in the Derwent Valley as dusk fell. For Charlotte, the White Lady had always been a legend in the back of her mind, but never a real possibility – until she was.

Signals

Once upon a time, the goal of modernisation was to have every town served by a railway station. In the Derwent Valley, the Nine Arches Viaduct runs for a hundred and fifty statuesque metres through the countryside, once a bypass to keep the regular trains out of the Gibside Estate – and now a monument to advances lost. Trains no longer pass through the valley. The local stations, like many nationwide, have long since been eradicated, and the tracks pulled up. But the railway bridges, or parts of them, remain, like little signals.

Charlotte, an experienced walker, has long relied on the skeletons of the railways to keep her tethered to the footpaths and byways. Below the heights of Gibside, the deep lanes of the valley are now shaped to the paths wrought by industry: if you follow the extinct railway line, you can't go far wrong. In the daytime, at least.

There are a lot of 'Derwents' in England. The word is a rare Brythonic relic, from *Derventio,* which means 'a valley thick with oak'. The Derwent Valley near Rowlands Gill is true to its name, densely treed and re-treed in the places where ancient forests were once torn down. Its hills are steep and its ravines precipitous; Charlotte had no intention of ever becoming trapped in the valley after nightfall.

Intention, unfortunately, does not always deliver reality.

The true impact of the earth's curvature between the north and south of a country as tiny as England can only be understood by those who've experienced the discrepancy of light in winter. Charlotte grew up in the north, but had spent most of her adult life in Hertfordshire. At home, it might have made sense to start a short hike at 3 p.m. on a mid-November day. In the north of England, with dusk falling twenty minutes earlier, this was foolhardy. But Charlotte had forgotten.

The Derwent Valley was at its best, all auburn leaves and trees shrinking beautifully against the lowering sun behind. Charlotte followed the railway path, and thought herself safe enough, in a world half-remembered and newly waymarked. Hollinside Manor glowered above; Charlotte ignored it in favour of a downward path into a thickly wooded valley. There were walkers with dogs still loping across the trail above. All was well.

The coming of dusk was strangely unexpected. It was that odd point in the year at which the world seems to lurch from one season to another, whole-bodied and brash. One moment, Charlotte was consulting her map; the next, she was blinking into the vague daylight, wondering where the sun had gone. The trees seemed to loom close around her. Charlotte swallowed, then got out her phone.

No signal – of course. Charlotte had recently extolled the virtues of Life360 to a friend: 'Look, it can place me within my own street! Within my house!' Here in the wilds of the valley, though, the signal was scattered by trees and hills and the neat little dot that was Charlotte told no true stories. Charlotte sighed, and put the useless thing away.

It wasn't as if she was lost. There was a vague sense of unease curling around her, certainly, but that was only natural. She'd strayed a little further into the forest than she'd meant. Now that she looked up, in the gathering gloom, she realised she'd left the path entirely.

No need to panic, of course. Charlotte took a breath, then turned her face up towards the skyline. In the distance, ragged branches stretched their limbs against the darkening sky. Charlotte squinted at the setting sun beyond, then lowered her face to the ground. The paths in this area were well-trodden and well-known. She would struggle to be truly lost.

One foot in front of the other, then. Charlotte focused on the ground, on the roots beneath her feet that might be her undoing.

The next time she glanced upwards, the dusky colour of the sky made her heart sink. It wasn't full darkness, but it was horrendously close. Charlotte pressed her lips together and tried to force her eyes to focus, searching for the clearly delineated paths in the hills above.

When the flash of white caught her eye, her first thought was that it was a hallucination, a hopeful little sparkle of substance in a dull and debilitating atmosphere. A sliver only; a spike of pale promise in the woods. Charlotte stilled, seeing it. Contained herself. The white flash was close by, that was for sure. A glimmer among the trees, like a distant hiker in pale garments, picking her way. Charlotte considered this – banked it against the fact of her poor eyesight – and began to move towards it.

The whiteness moved. As Charlotte shifted carefully down paths that were not paths, the white flash shifted in front of her, bold and purposeful. Occasionally, it would pause, as if considering, but then would strike out in a new direction, always beneath the treeline, around the ruined mill. It was no footpath they were following, Charlotte realised. This was a way out of the valley unknown to the National Trust.

Eventually, the flash of white skittered hopefully leftwards and Charlotte followed, until a black-painted gatepost was seen. When Charlotte reached it, she realised she knew where she was: the Derwent Walk, once the railway line, was in front of her, stretching ahead smoothly into the twilight. The white flash was gone, Charlotte noticed. Her panic was gone, too.

When the thudding of her heart had calmed, she let herself look up at the hill above, still thickly covered in oak trees. Halfway up, she saw a woman in a white dress, eyeing her with something close to smugness. She wasn't ethereal or ghostly. She didn't even appear melan-choly. The Woman in White – the peripatetic glimmer Charlotte had been watching – was young, ordinarily pretty, and soft-eyed, her dark hair framing a warm and hopeful face.

Charlotte's gaze held the green eyes for a long moment, then looked away as if to recalibrate herself. When she looked back, there was nothing there but the trees.

*

A key element in many stories of the Gibside White Lady is that she is benign, benevolent, determined. One of us. One of the most frequently told tales is that she is seen in a white carriage, escaping the villain who tried to keep her captive in the castle. Boys picking potatoes in the fields outside Gibside have watched her leave, and she lifted a pale hand in salute. My grandfather, as I mentioned earlier, claimed to have witnessed the carriage, alongside numerous friends. Implicit in this tale is a sense of sympathy for the fleeing spirit which, nevertheless, spares the ghost from victimhood. She is celebrated for leaving a plight any woman must. It is this part of Mary Eleanor's story which has endured, and not her infidelities, nor any of the shocking reputations that dogged her in life.

The White Lady of Gibside, like many such spirits, has become so embedded in the local community that only about half of my tale-tellers knew 'the real story', beyond having a general idea of her as a woman in flight from evil. But it is difficult not to find scraps of it in the way the Lady presents herself today – in the way she is seen and expected to be seen. Children walking in the

Derwent Valley are still encouraged to keep an eye out for a flash of white in the trees, a sign that the White Lady is roaming abroad. Andrew Stoney might have locked her in her home, but he and the home have gone now, and the woods are the White Lady's playground. The sight of her raises goosebumps, but she has as much right to the land as the living.

The White Lady of Gibside – or that part of her that was once Mary Eleanor – might easily have been called a child-murderess and, in her lifetime, she frequently was. Fragments of cultural memory of these events do survive in local lore, but they seem to have been split off from the core tale of the spirit. Instead, these elements have become part of a living belief in witchcraft, which the next chapter of this book will explore.

The White Lady spirit, meanwhile, is not a vengeful or dangerous one. On the contrary, she is a feature of the local landscape who both protects and is to be protected – something echoed in a similar tale from St Michael's Mount in Cornwall, four hundred miles away.

Causeway

In winter, no ferries run between the Cornish mainland and St Michael's Mount. The only route back from the island to neighbouring Marazion is the ancient, cobbled causeway, accessible only when the tide is low. Stephen was painfully aware of this as, one November day in 1997, he hurried towards the checkpoint. His watch read 4.03 and, this late in the year, the dusk was fast falling. The causeway closed at 4.35 p.m. If he didn't make it in time, he would be stranded, as a tour guide had cautioned that morning, adding, 'Jack the Giant will get you.'

Stephen didn't believe in Jack the Giant, but he *did* believe that being stranded on the island overnight would be unpleasant and inconvenient.

A landscape artist, Stephen had grown up in nearby Penzance and was no stranger to the Mount. On the contrary, it compelled him, his artist's eye struck by its majesty, its crags and curlicues, and the hulking castle at its crest. Paintings of the Mount sold well, too, to postcard companies and in tourist emporiums. As darkness crept in, the castle limned in sunset colours could often look especially stunning, and it was his effort to capture this effect that had led Stephen to dally too long. The tide was drawing in.

On a quiet night, so the fishermen said, the water brought with it the sound of church bells ringing. If you listened closely, you might even hear the last promise of poor hanged Sarah Polgrean to her lover Jack: 'I will, I will . . .' Sarah was hanged at Bodmin Gaol in 1820, by all accounts rightly, having poisoned her husband with arsenic. Local folklore, however, preferred to linger on the more romantic aspect of the story, her voice on the wind intermingled with the sounds of lost villages now fathoms deep.

Stephen had never heard the bells. Fishermen were a superstitious lot; it would turn anyone's brain, Stephen thought, to live so much at the whims and mercy of the sea. What concerned him more was the fact that his painting wasn't finished. He held it away from his body as he walked, hoping to preserve it from any scuffs. When he reached the checkpoint at the base of the island, it was 4.18 p.m. Just about enough time to cross, if he walked fast.

Darkness continued to fall. In the summer months, the Mount drew thousands of visitors a day, but on this November evening, licked with frost, Stephen was almost alone. At the far end of the causeway, one intrepid family was just disappearing onto the mainland, reaching safe harbour. Stephen watched them go and felt a prickle of unease beneath the collar of his heavy coat. The water was drawing in, and there he stood, a solitary figure in the middle of the causeway.

He wasn't sure what made him turn. One moment, he was acutely aware of his loneliness, standing like the last man at the edge of the world, as the waters drew in. The next, he was convinced there was somebody with him. Something like a breath curled against the back of his neck: far, far too warm to be the wind on an afternoon like this.

Stephen turned at once, his heart leaping into his throat. The causeway, of course, was empty. Stephen clutched at his chest, willing himself to calm. It was only his nerves; only the lateness of the hour and the oppressiveness of the quiet. No wonder the fishermen heard bells.

Pausing for a moment, he took in the island. The castle was a vast silhouette against the sky; the light had changed considerably since he'd packed up his things. There would be no finishing the painting tonight.

Just as he was about to turn away, he noticed a figure high up on the battlements, stiff-backed and still. That would make an arresting painting, he thought. It was the figure of a woman, dressed in white, her long dark hair hanging loose around her face. The face itself, at this distance, was indistinct. Stephen fumbled in his pocket for a disposable camera, intending to snap a quick shot for reference. He withdrew the camera and clicked. When he lowered it, the figure was gone.

Stephen shook his head as if to clear it; looked again. The place where the figure had been was definitely empty. Stephen remembered the warm breath on his neck, but – no, he told himself. The castle was inhabited, after all. The figure had probably been a teenage daughter of the family. Teenagers move quickly, except when they're determined not to move at all. He was being silly. Still, he picked up his pace as he continued towards the mainland. No man ever won in a battle against the tides.

In Marazion, his car was where he'd left it in the long stay car park. For all his bluster, it was with a sense of deep relief that he unlocked the driver's side door and slid into his seat. The car park, like the causeway, was deserted; when Stephen turned the key in the ignition, the radio roared to life along with the engine. The familiar sound of Oasis helped slow Stephen's heart rate.

Then came a rap on the window.

Stephen stilled. He thought of the bells, and sad Sarah's last promise, and the fishermen, and felt as he turned his head that he'd rather have bells on the silent waters than this, the empty car park and the strident tapping on his window.

A girl stood there, white-faced and impassive. Her hair was long and dark, loose around her face, and her dress was bridal white. What struck Stephen most of all was the certainty in her gaze as they looked at each other. For what felt like forever, the girl looked at Stephen, unspeaking, and Stephen looked back. He could do nothing else.

Eventually – as if spurred by some cue Stephen could not hear – she straightened. She walked away. Stephen was almost unsurprised to see her disappear by the exit barriers, as if melting into the darkness. It was as if he had lost the capacity to feel surprise; or perhaps simply that he had known already that this would happen. The girl would disappear, as she had before on the battlements. Stephen closed his eyes and forced himself to breathe again.

He felt little surprise, either, when the photographs were developed and his study of the girl on the battlements showed only battlements, and no girl. He painted the image anyway and, with great care, put her back in it.

*

St Michael's Mount is reputedly one of the most haunted places in Cornwall. In many ways, it could hardly help being so. All the traditional elements of the ghost story are there. The vast castle is still inhabited by the same family, the St Aubyns, who bought it shortly after the English Civil War. The fourteenth-century church stands on the footprint of one built in 1135. And the island itself has been considered a place of spirituality from the fifth century, when the archangel Michael supposedly appeared on the shore to guide fishermen safely home. Today, ley lines which cross under the heart of the Mount make it a lure for New Agers who believe in the Mount's healing properties as strongly as their medieval predecessors did.

What is interesting about Stephen's story – told to me as absolutely true – is that it seems to roll together two more frequently recounted stories of White Ladies in the vicinity of the Mount. Traditionally, the Mount itself is haunted by a 'grey lady' believed to be the spirit of a nanny who served the St Aubyn family in the 1750s. Whether a lady is 'grey' or 'white' seems to be largely immaterial; the idea of the spirit being grey seems to reflect the way she is perceived, as through a mist. Her clothing is usually described as being white. Like Gibside's White Lady, this is a woman who has suffered in love. Unmarried and pregnant, the unhappy nanny is alleged to have thrown herself from the battlements of the castle when her lover refused to marry her. Also, like Gibside's White Lady, this one is benign, sympathetic, and very much a victim. Frequently seen in her final fall from the battlements, the Grey Lady can neither be helped nor help herself.

The other story is that of the White Lady of Marazion. On Marazion Green, so the story goes, a white lady is seen to leap onto the back of a gentleman's horse and ride with him, sometimes as far as the Red River. Unsettling tales have been told of this woman catching up with stage-coaches and, more recently, cars, and riding level with them, meeting the drivers' eyes. Her gaze is said to be penetrating, challenging. No identity has been mooted for this woman, although it has been pointed out that the spot where she appears is near where Sir John Arundell, Sheriff of Cornwall, was killed whilst leading an attack on St Michael's Mount in 1471.

In Stephen's story, the women are one and the same. The implications of this seem to represent a fascinating lens into how our ghosts grow and change with us. Stephen was adamant that he did not believe in the fishermen's legends of bells at sea: these were, in his mind, tales from the past, understandable means by which a community of fishermen sustained and consoled themselves. To him, these tales were nothing but ancient lore. But a White Lady is an acceptable ghost, even for a person who is not among the thousands in Cornwall who attend spiritualist churches and keep a psychic medium on speed dial. She is based in and reinforced by the community: presumed to have been a part of it in life, her role within it is sustained for as long as people expect to catch a pale glimpse of her, or tell ever-shifting versions of her story by pub firesides. A White Lady is the sort of ghost a right-thinking person can allow themselves to see.

In the older stories, the poor Grey Lady of St Michael's Mount meets a lamentable end. She has been wronged, yes, but there's also an element of punishment implied in the way she is doomed to repeat her death fall, over and over again. The White Lady of Marazion Green is an entirely different character, riding furiously for her freedom and meeting men's eyes as she does it, as if in challenge. In Stephen's account, the Grey Lady is somehow trans-figured into the White one, becoming more powerful in the process – much like Tolkien's Gandalf the Grey becoming the almost-omnipotent Gandalf the White after his battle with the Balrog. The stories blur together, repres-enting a shift in perceptions of femininity. The Grey Lady remains benevolent, but now she is triumphantly so, no longer content simply to die endlessly for her mistakes. The princess saves herself, and we applaud it.

This is why, ultimately, the so-called identity of the ghost is less important than the identity (and beliefs) of the perceiver. We reinvent ourselves through our stories, as people have always done.

The stagecoach and horses appear in many White Lady stories, far beyond the Gibside and Marazion ones. White Ladies, it seems, are frequently seen in transit.

One interesting modern example comes from rural Tyrone, Northern Ireland, where a mysterious White Lady made headlines nationwide in 2009. Hundreds of visitors flocked to the isolated country road at Mullaghmoyle near Coalisland, where locals claimed a ghost had been 'stirred up' by the felling of a fairy tree. Many had seen the ghost before, but the recent spate of hauntings had been unusually virulent.

News reports from the time suggested that the locals were more disturbed by the influx of press attention than by the ghost, which local youth Paul Corr dismissed as 'nothing great'. The matter-of-fact reaction to the presence of the ghost itself reflected the attitudes of those in northern England who called Northumbria Police about their ghost troubles: the ghost was an irritation, but of course it was real. The landlord of the Four Corners pub near the place where the woman was seen claimed to have spotted her 'about twenty times'. Warren Coates, founder of the Northern Ireland Paranormal Research Association, observed that they had received multiple reports of paranormal activity in the location since the mid-1980s.

One man explained to the Belfast *Telegraph* that the fairy tree had contained a 'bottled spirit' and should never have been cut down:

'It was a common thing round here. The local priest would have come round, exorcised a place and put the spirit in a bottle.

'Then a tree would have been planted so that it would never be disturbed, but that tree was cut down recently.'

If this is the case, however, then the spirit must have undergone something of a metamorphosis in its bottle, as the White Lady reported in 2009 had an interest in something not much known in spirit-bottling days – namely: cars and their drivers.

The Bend in the Road

At first, Colm thought the figure by the side of the road was his mother. He related this almost apologetically to a group who perfectly understood the reason for Colm's embarrassment. Grace Ferguson had died some months before, and her spirit had left her body, Colm would say, almost a year before that. Before she went into the nursing home, Grace was more than once found wandering in the dark, her hair loose around her face and her nightdress flapping like a white sail at the roadside. More than once, Colm had driven a lonely road like this one, looking for his mother.

Now, though, Grace was gone, and as Colm approached the bend in the Mullaghmoyle Road near the farmhouse that had been crumbling for years, he felt a knot form in his stomach.

At the side of the road, getting clearer and clearer as the car drew closer, stood the figure of a woman.

In rural County Tyrone – as in much of the rest of the United Kingdom – the country roads are unlit. A misty, drizzling rain obfuscated visibility still further, but the figure stood silhouetted in the clear arcs of Colm's head-lights, dark hair loose, white dress flapping around its thin legs.

As Colm approached, the figure held out its arm. The thumb was held aloft, in the universal language of the hitchhiker: *Please stop for me.*

Colm did not want to stop. At the back of his mind, however, a small, sensible voice said: *This could be someone else's mother, wandering the dark roads and the still-darker recesses of her own mind. Ought to stop, Colm. Ought to stop and be sure.*

Fighting every impulse, Colm slowed the car further. Water sluiced up from the ditch at the edge of the road as he came to a halt. The figure turned its head towards him.

Where its face should have been, there was nothing. Or perhaps an impression of nothingness – as Colm put it, 'like static on your television'.

Colm wasted no time in pulling away from the verge. It felt as if every organ in his body had been pulled up into his throat, his heart pounded furiously. He'd heard chatter in the pub about restless spirits, but had always put it down to spirits of another kind. Now, Colm raced away from the offending spot as fast as he could, his whole body vibrating.

He didn't know, he said, whether the figure disappeared after that. He'd whipped round the hairpin bend far too fast to look back and check.

*

If the White Lady of the Mullaghmoyle Road was once, as the landlord suggested, a spirit crammed into a bottle by some long-ago priest, then she must have spent her time in confinement watching cult teen movies. This story is interesting within the catalogue of White Ladies in the British Isles for a number of reasons. First of all, like the

White Lady of Gibside, the presence of this woman is considered almost a matter of local record. She appears to a community where acceptance of ghosts – and even, perhaps, fairy trees in which to confine them – is high. Secondly, unlike other White Ladies, the appearance of this particular spirit over the past several decades seems unconnected to any particular ghost of times gone by. She is often called a White Lady, but the way she appeared from the 1980s – when Warren Coates first recorded sighting reports – took a very 1980s form, which blends the White Lady with another, semi-connected type of ghost.

As Coates put it, many of his reports related to 'a phantom female hitchhiker, who caused a stir some years ago . . . Drivers would see her on the side of the road with her thumb out. When they pulled up to offer her a lift, she would vanish.'

'The Vanishing Hitchhiker' is a type of ghost story or urban legend which gained particular popularity after the 1981 publication of Jan Harold Brunvand's so-titled book. While Brunvand notes that versions of the story can be traced back to the 1870s, the majority of sightings date from the twentieth century, beginning in the United States. The core of the story is that a driver stops to pick up a hitchhiker, almost invariably a woman, who either vanishes from a moving vehicle or is discovered later to have been a deceased person.

The Mullaghmoyle story does not fit properly into any of the categories of Vanishing Hitchhiker identified by folklorists Richard Beardsley and Rosalie Hankey in the early 1940s. She does not . . .

1. give an address which betrays her ghostly nature;
2. appear as an old woman prophesying disaster;
3. seek a lift from somebody, and then leave her coat behind in the car; *or*
4. transpire to have been a local divinity.

The Mullaghmoyle woman, most importantly of all, never gets into anyone's car, nor does she leave a token behind. However, like many Vanishing Hitchhikers (and unlike many British White Ladies), she is often described as an elderly lady rather than a young one. Like most Hitchhikers, she tends to seek the attention of a male driver. And like other well-known roadside spirits, such as the White Woman of the Bölchentunnel in Switzerland, she began creating a nuisance in the early 1980s – almost as if the ghosts had read Brunvand's book.

A certain sense of sympathy for the spirit is something which, interestingly, seems to define many true British White Lady stories – something not always true of analogous tales from abroad. Japanese *yūrei,* with their long dark hair and shroud-like white attire, have been most popularised in the West in the form of female 'vengeful' ghosts, their purpose in returning to earth often violent. *La Llorona* of Mexico has historically also been a vengeful ghost, a child-murderess punished for her crimes by being forced to wander the earth for eternity, weeping.

In Mexico, her story is often used as a warning to children: do not wander off into the dark alone, or *La Llorona* will get you.

Today, in the same way that social change has encouraged new interpretations of White Ladies, *La Llorona* is being reconsidered by modern folklorists and feminists. We now appreciate that this legend – the vengeful ghost who drowned her own children and is consequently forced to roam wailing in the dark – has a patriarchal root: it is a warning for women not to stray from the paths set out for them. And yet, important though it is to perform these re-examinations, the fact remains that *La Llorona* is a wholly unpleasant character. Not content to kill her own children, she also kills other women's. In response, supposedly, to her own husband's violence, she enacts and re-enacts that violence herself. *La Llorona* is a malevolent, terrifying spectre.

White Ladies, even where the perception of them does reflect sexist views, are rarely presented so misogynistically. Infanticide, drownings and curses are, in the UK, generally the preserve of another type of being entirely.

It's undoubtedly true that the less appealing traits of Mary Eleanor Bowes, the Unhappy Countess, seem to have been largely forgotten in the echo of her that walks the Derwent Valley in the form of the White Lady. However, that is not to say that elements of the Banshee, the *cyhyraeth,* and *La Llorona* herself are not believed to haunt the same spaces, in another version of the same woman – simply wearing a different dress.

In the Woods

When I was a child, I was always warned that the woods behind my parents' house were where the witches gathered. I never questioned this. Sometimes, when hastening home through the trees as twilight fell, I'd see cairns arranged in circular formation, silent little sentinels of stone. Obviously, they were man-made – or rather, witch-made. That seemed logical enough. Today, I wonder whether perhaps some intrepid parent was behind the cairns, hoping to bolster the stories of witches we told at sleepovers with torches held under our chins. It's easier, perhaps, to keep teenagers out of the woods because they fear a midnight coven than because there are other, wholly explicable, dangers that might befall them. One way or another, there *are* evil things in our woods and wildernesses: perhaps witches cling on to modern communities as a representation of those evils which children can easily understand.

In my home community, though, as in many all over the British Isles, belief in witches is not confined to children. In the Derwent Valley, witches are whispered to have once roamed abroad, abducting children in the thick of the forest and drowning babies in the shallow river. As a child, I took these stories for granted. It was only when I began researching the ghosts of the British Isles that I began to see the similarities – and the differences – between these spectres and the White Ladies who walk alongside them, often occupying the same physical spaces in entirely different ways. Today, the White Lady of Gibside Hall is a version of Mary Eleanor Bowes in line with modern mores, a brave and laudable woman. Perhaps the witches and witch-ghosts of the Derwent Valley, though, are part of Mary Eleanor, too – sinister splinters of her which no longer feel in keeping with the benevolent community spirit. One particular example springs to mind . . .

Cry-by-Night

In the 1990s, Susan kept The Red Kite pub, then The Golden Lion. The pub, previously mentioned, stands in the bottom of the valley, below the old railway arch, with Gibside Estate stretching up the great looming green hill behind. At the top of the hill, the stately 'Column to Liberty' broadcasts the lofty position of the estate for miles around. This is right in the heart of Mary Eleanor's territory.

Susan is a professional landlord; she also believes herself to be, as she put it to me, 'susceptible'. In another pub she lived in, she had 'company', a presence that would manifest as a blonde woman glimpsed out of the corner of an eye and whose favourite trick was to pull out the plug in the bathtub while Susan was in it. Cupboard doors would open and close. Snatches of laughter would materialise out of nowhere, the unknown breath that formed them causing Susan's stomach to drop warily and strands of her hair to move. This spectre, though, Susan insisted, felt mostly harmless. The presence she encountered at The Golden Lion was a different, more troubling matter.

'If it had been *in* the pub,' Susan admitted, 'I wouldn't have stayed.'

But the presence wasn't in the pub – not exactly.

The disturbances began very quickly after Susan took up residence. One night, she remembers, she was woken in the small hours by what could only be described as distant wailing.

She scrambled for her bedside clock: 3.30 a.m. The witching hour, Susan thought, and then laughed at herself for the way her body went cold in reaction. Probably foxes. Anybody who has ever heard their furious night-time couplings will know how uncannily human they can sound. Susan pulled the pillow over her head and tried to blot out the sound.

To her dismay, however, the sounds seemed to be moving towards, rather than away from, the back of the pub.

The garden behind the building is small; a narrow stream provides a natural boundary at the bottom of it. Beyond the stream, fields give way to woods. Susan had never heard mating foxes *moving* like this before – seemingly, counterproductively, in the middle of the act. Warily, she removed the pillow.

As soon as she had done so, she felt immediately frozen in her bed. Great, gasping wails drifted in through her half-open window, interspersed with unmistakable sobs. These were wails of agony; of desperation; of a person in peril. As the sounds drew nearer and nearer, Susan made out a shuddering gasp and then a devastated, devastating cry: 'My baby!'

Susan immediately bolted out of bed. Later, she would put it down to base human instinct; the voice was too close and too clear for fears of the unknown to let her ignore someone in potential peril. She rushed to the window. There, by the stream, was the vague but definite pale shape of a person. Susan swore, fumbled for the light switch, and rushed downstairs.

As she hastily donned her wellies and coat over her pyjamas, she ran frantically through her next steps in her mind. A young mother, maybe, intoxicated or on drugs? A tragic accident? Perhaps it wasn't too late to save the baby, if there was one. She ran down the path through the beer garden with her heart thumping, torch in hand.

'Who's there?' she called as she ran. 'I'm going to help you. Do we need to call an ambulance?'

In the thick winter night, the garden, little-used since the summer, lay still and empty. Only when Susan made it to the stream did she realise the wailing must have stopped as she was rushing out of the house. The garden was empty: no mother, and no baby.

Well, Susan tried to tell herself, *good.* It was good that nobody was injured. It was good that nobody was there.

Just as she got back into bed, though, the sobbing began again.

This, Susan said, was a pattern that was to repeat itself several times during her tenure at the pub. It wasn't every night, or close to every night, but she heard the wailing woman at least two or three times a year – although she never again ventured outside to render assistance.

85

Eventually she mentioned it to some of her patrons, curious as to whether anyone else had heard the keening.

'Someone told me the pub was built on a white witches' coven,' Susan said, 'which then became a black witches' coven. There was a sort of fight between them, and a black witch murdered a white witch's baby.'

Did Susan believe that?

'There's no evidence of the coven,' she said, shrugging, 'but someone's there.'

*

There is a strange connection between wailing women, witches and water. Like the Welsh *cyhyraeth*, these so-called witches behind The Golden Lion wail and moan in the night and materialise near bodies of water. Like *La Llorona*, they prey on children. It's interesting that local patrons did not conflate *this* white figure with the area's most famous spectral inhabitant. Perhaps while our White Ladies have come to symbolise wounded or triumphant womanhood, it is in our witches, and our witch-ghosts, that society's most misogynistic archetypes continue to be expressed. The White Lady of Gibside Hall would not endanger children as Mary Eleanor, at the nadir of her popularity, was said to do – but a witch might. Despite all the advances in surveillance technology and forensic science, children disappear every day without a trace. Why not let a witch take the blame? And why not make a distinction between White Ladies, those Acceptable

Modern Ghosts, and their unsavoury witch counterparts, the embodiment of our more primal prejudices and fears?

All societies, even as they change, need a villain at whose door they can lay their troubles. Most of us know the story of Matthew Hopkins, the so-called Witchfinder General, and his successful whipping of sixteenth-century para-noiacs into a witch-hunting frenzy. Witches, he convinced his followers, were the root of all social evil. Today, we like to think we are more enlightened than our ancestors, who laid the blame for all social issues at the feet of their unpalatable women: their elderly, their unmarried, their eccentric and their adulterous. And yet, there are certain crimes which, when enacted by a woman, are deemed especially unforgivable to this day. When the Moors murderers, Ian Brady and Myra Hindley, were captured by police in 1965, Brady was rightly condemned as an appalling and inhuman creature – but it was Hindley who was branded 'the most evil woman in Britain'. The press's approach suggested that while a man murdering children is tragic, a woman doing so is innately more monstrous. As an unnamed elderly lady staunchly told BBC news cameras in 1966: 'A bad man's a bad man, but a bad woman's a *bloody* bad woman.'

Of course, horror at mistreatment of children, of any kind and by anyone, is an attitude which does not and should not change, whatever the morals of the society in which we live. The elderly lady's attitude, however, is one which has been held down the centuries in far more innocuous scenarios – and, indeed, where a man would not have been thought culpable of any transgression at all. Eccentricity, disobedience, and even plain rudeness were all misdemeanours which saw women condemned to death as witches by Matthew Hopkins – treated exactly as if they had been child-murderers.

It is interesting, then, that the stories we tell about today's witches continue to revolve around archetypes and anxieties older even than the language of these Isles. Our White Ladies may have been forgiven their trespasses, but our witches abduct, assault and murder in their stead, remaining a distinctly female threat to our children, our safety and our social order. Statistically, it might be men who are more likely to abduct and murder our children in the dark, but it's women we fear the most in such a circumstance; and Bad Women whose shadows stretch longest across even the most modern of lives.

We are not yet a post-feminist society. We still believe in bad women – and in witches. In the next chapter, we'll look at how witches have endured across the British Isles, not only as flesh and blood covens in the woods, but also as spectres embodying our changing and unchanging fears.

Chapter Three
Rumours of Witches

IN MID-2019, I bought a house in rural North Oxfordshire. The village I live in, like 231 other parishes in Oxfordshire, is home to fewer than a thousand people. It's the sort of place where the houses have thatched roofs and names which are relics of an earlier tongue; with nary a number in sight, any unaccustomed postman has his work cut out for him. In many ways, a time-traveller from the sixteenth century could find herself in an Oxfordshire village and spot nothing amiss, not least because many of the county's most rural inhabitants are too elderly or too busy to bother with such nuisances as smartphones.

There are many other places in the United Kingdom, of course, where the same time-traveller would be equally untroubled. In the wild mountains of Snowdonia, or among the purple heather of the Scottish Highlands, hiking through Northumberland National Park or perambulating in the Peak District, it is impossible not to stop and recognise that our ancestors might have stood where we now stand, and seen nothing different. The ancient elements that persist in our landscapes are, in many cases, evidence of civilisations so far removed from us in time that they would have been as mysterious and profound to our time-traveller as they are to us today.

The anonymous Anglo-Saxon poem, 'Deor', refers to the ruins of Roman monuments as *enta geweorc,* or 'the work of giants'. J. R. R. Tolkien, whose fictional Shire was an idealised Oxfordshire, borrowed this word, *enta,* and applied it to his race of ancient forest beings, the Ents, old enough to remember the earliest marks man made upon the landscape. From the Rollright Stones in the north to the Uffington White Horse in the south, Oxfordshire is replete with *enta geweorc.* We don't know, and probably will never know, why these features were first developed, or by whom. We don't know why a vast animal figure was cut into the chalk hills above the vale now named for the White Horse. For centuries, however, it has been assumed that whoever created the horse had good reason to do so. In the Welsh *Red Book of Hergest,* written in the late fourteenth or early fifteenth century, it is said of the White Horse that 'nothing grows upon it', and for many hundreds of years, the locals made sure that this was the case. The Scouring of the White Horse took place ceremonially every seven years until the late nineteenth century, with the markings only knowingly covered during the Second World War, to prevent them being used as a navigational beacon by the Luftwaffe. Now the National Trust organises scourings as family days out. We don't know what the White Horse does, but we assume it does *something*. Best to keep it clean, just in case – while hoping that whichever strange god the horse appeases will be understanding of a little problem like Hitler. This is the sort of rock upon which all superstition is built. Like standing stones, these rocks endure for centuries, leaving our rural landscapes littered with the corpses of long-dead gods to whom many still perform obeisance – just in case.

It's not only arcane prehistoric beliefs, though, to which we still unwittingly nod. There's a particular tree whose powers of protection have remained close to the pragmatic forefront of folk-wisdom and casual superstition. When I was three years old, I helped my father plant a rowan tree in our garden. He said it would keep the witches away, an idea which, rather than comforting me, filled me with deep anxiety that the tree might also repel Santa Claus. At that time, I wasn't particularly anxious about witches. Nor was my father, but his unschooled understanding of the rowan's meaning speaks to the fact that, not so many generations ago, many people were. As one Scots rhyme puts it, 'Rowan tree and red threed/ Makes the witches tyne their speed'. If you inspect a rowan berry, you will find opposite its stalk a tiny five-pointed star, a pentagram of the sort that shielded Good Gawain from evil in the *Morte D'Arthur*. The vibrant red berries erupt in shocking profusion in autumn; red, the colour of blood and livelihood, has long been considered the best protection against malevolent magic. These two accidents of nature combine to make the rowan tree an obvious witch-repellent. Driving down the deep lanes of Oxfordshire in October, the frequency of rowan trees suggests that the issue of witches was once a very significant concern indeed.

It's easy to assume that, in twenty-first-century Britain, witches are about as pressing an issue as bubonic plague or Bigfoot. While a significant number of people will readily answer 'yes' to the question of whether or not they believe in ghosts, very few said the same when I asked if they believed in witches. Significantly, however, they didn't say *no*. In twenty-first-century Britain, this is, instead, a question to be answered with a question. What kind of witch? A bad witch, or a good one? A Wiccan practitioner, or something more like the Wicked Witch of the West?

Whether or not we believe in witches depends entirely on what a witch is, and what we mean when we use the term. There's nothing new there, though. The meaning of a word like 'witch' changes as we move through geography and time, depending on social mores, community concerns and systems of belief. A witch might be human, post-human, sub-human; they might be spirit or flesh, male or female, good or evil.

What does the word 'witch' mean in the twenty-first century? Is there any sort of consensus about what constitutes a witch at all?

It's a fair question – and, as in many other arenas, one which is impossible to answer without considering the routes witches and witchcraft have taken, in Britain in particular, to reach their current cultural position. To understand the present, the best thing we can do is to first look to the past – to the point in time when witches made their greatest mark upon British society. Our modern conception of witches would have been significantly different were it not for the prolonged, frenetic and horrifying time of the Witch Trials – which did not fully come to an end until alarmingly recently. It's little wonder we can still hear the echoes.

Tring Air

Tring Woodlands in Hertfordshire is a well-established, semi-natural site whose abundant beech, ash and oak trees would have looked little different in the eighteenth century from the way they look today. Under the lush canopy of trees grow the sorts of wild flora whose names taste like witchcraft in the mouth: dog's mercury; wood sanicle; white helleborine. The woods are dark, richly green, a favourite haunt of dogwalkers and day-ramblers. In the 1990s, Stacey and her friend Emma took frequent advantage of the green space as a place to exercise their horses and Emma's two large collies, Shep and Sarah.

The dogs loved the woods. So did the two young women. On spring afternoons, the sun filtered yellow through the canopy of leaves and the air was rich with the scents of moss and rain. Although the site was a popular one, its vastness meant they were usually undisturbed. Occasionally the cracking of twigs in the undergrowth would signal an approaching couple, or a family with their dog. More often than not, the woods were gloriously silent, but for the rushing of the wind in the trees.

In this silence, the distant sound of marching feet on an April afternoon was very loud indeed.

It began out of nowhere. At first, as Stacey brought her horse to a halt, she thought she must be imagining it – or else misinterpreting one sound for another. It was still full daylight, birds chirping gaily overhead. Stacey held her breath, the better to listen.

There was no mistaking it. Somewhere far away, but swiftly approaching, were feet tramping through the undergrowth. Multiple, steady, syncopated marching feet.

The horses' ears had pricked up. This emboldened Stacey to look across and catch Emma's eye. 'Can you hear . . .?'

'Shh.' Emma cocked her head. In this attentive pose, she resembled the collies, both of whom were also intently listening. Nervously, Stacey curled her fingers more tightly around the horse's reins.

'Someone's coming,' she said, when she could bear it no longer. Emma frowned.

'Maybe there's something on,' she suggested. 'We might have missed it. Some sort of – re-enactment, or . . .?'

Evidently, imagination failed her as to what the *something* might be. Stacey swallowed anxiously. The sound of the mob – she used the word automatically; something about the footsteps was too ugly to signify anything else – was coming closer. As she squinted through the trees, Stacey thought they should surely now be close enough to see. The dogs and the horses all stood stock-still, ears pricked, eyes trained in the same direction.

Nearer came the mob. Nearer, nearer. The animals' eyes didn't move – until they did.

The sound was almost on top of them now. As it reached fever pitch, the dogs began to bark. Their gaze shifted from the left, scanning slowly across the trees as the churning of mud and the tramping of boots reached the women – and passed them. There was no denying it. A noisy, relentless party of people was making its thunderous way through the clearing, not ten feet from where Stacey and Emma stood. It just so happened that only the dogs and the horses could see them.

The sound faded away into the distance. The dogs watched the group until, seemingly, they could no longer be seen. Into the dusky woods the footsteps died away, not immediately, but naturally, the way any footsteps would. The footsteps were real enough. It was only the steppers who were unusual. Stacey felt something run down her spine like cold water.

Eventually, the dogs lost interest. Shep began nuzzling insouciantly at a stick, which gave Stacey the courage to move. She tugged again at the horse's reins, more to soothe herself than anything, and smiled shakily at Emma.

'Shall we go?' she asked.

'God,' said Emma, 'yes. Come on, quick, before they come back.'

They didn't discuss who *they* might be. Stacey was glad. She didn't think she could stand to hear any suggestions.

*

Stacey and Emma are far from the only people to have experienced a mob marching near Tring. Some say they're soldiers. Others, who describe the presence as near-suffocatingly ominous, have offered alternative explanations. More than once in Tring, a mob took it upon itself to hunt an alleged witch to extinction. Perhaps the woods still carry the imprints of their fear – or their malice. What goes around, comes around, or so they say. Do the woods resonate with the aftermath of witchy evildoing – or did the people of early modern Hertfordshire, so keen to violently ostracise their unwanted women, create an eternal karmic prison for themselves?

It's often claimed that Hertfordshire saw England's last witch trial. Certainly, the county seemed to exhibit a particular passion for prosecuting its citizens under the witchcraft laws, first passed in 1542 by Henry VIII. The first recorded prosecution for witchcraft in Hertfordshire took place in 1573, and a further ninety-six indictments followed. The last one, that of Jane Wenham of Walkern in 1712, was broadly similar to most of its antecedents. Jane, a single woman in her seventies, was charged with using witchcraft to kill local cattle and horses. Jane was vulnerable and by all accounts unpopular; the fact that the trial judge, Sir John Powell, quite clearly felt the accusations against her were unfounded did not deter the jury from sentencing Jane to death. Powell stayed the execution, seeking a royal pardon. Evidently, however, it was greatly feared that locals would take matters into their own hands; Jane was taken into the protection of a Captain John Plummer 'that she might not afterward be torn to peeces [*sic*]'.

Like most witch stories of this era, Jane's saga was rooted in suspicion, misogyny and petty local politics. In January 1712, Jane came to John Chapman's farm and asked for a pennyworth of straw from Chapman's servant, Matthew Gilston. Rather than giving her straw from his master's barn, Matthew – for some reason – felt compelled to run to a farm several miles away, where he first asked for some straw and, being refused it, travelled further until he found some on a dung heap, which he carried home.

Matthew's odd behaviour seems to have been sufficient for Chapman – who had long been convinced that Jane was the cause of illness in his cattle and horses – to label her 'a Witch and Bitch'. Jane protested to the magistrate, crying slander. This, for a woman in her position, was a grave misstep.

Things quickly went from bad to worse. Now obligated to investigate the alleged slander, Sir Henry Chauncy, the magistrate, 'heard . . . very ill' of Jane. Chauncy referred the case to the Reverend Gardiner, and the whole matter could then have been resolved had Jane been satisfied with Gardiner's recommendation that Chapman pay Jane a shilling in compensation. Jane was not satisfied. The dispute worsened.

The reverend's maidservant, Anne, seems to have fallen foul of Jane's displeasure after the judgement. In early February, she claimed that Jane had caused 'a strange Roaming in her Head', implying witchcraft. Jane warned the girl against telling further 'Stories' about her, suggesting that she would suffer if she did. Anne promptly claimed to have been overcome with pain, convulsions, and a compulsion to immerse herself in the river. Jane was subsequently arrested for witchcraft. She could not (or, perhaps, would not) recite the Lord's Prayer. On 16 February, she confessed to having bewitched Anne and to have entered into a pact with the Devil some sixteen years previously. One can only guess at the circumstances which might have produced such a confession. Her execution stayed, Jane seems to have died in due course of old age, but Plummer's anxiety that she might be 'torn to peeces' suggests that the people of Tring had form. History bears this out.

Jane's was the last official trial under the witchcraft laws in Hertfordshire, but it was by no means the last trial by mob. Arthur MacDonald, in his irreverent 1941 *A Gossiping and Irresponsible History of Tring,* blames 'that Tring Air' for the persistence of a 'universal belief in witchcraft' until the mid-eighteenth century in the area. He records a 1751 instance in which a disease among cattle – almost certainly foot and mouth disease – was blamed on an old woman, Ruth Osborn, who seems to have been of a similar temperament to her predecessor Jane Wenham. The cattle farmer recalled having once refused her buttermilk, upon which she cursed him, saying: 'I hope the Pretender will come and take your pigs, and you, too.' Ruth was outspoken and unpopular. It was enough.

No longer able to take their case to the courts, the people of Tring dragged Ruth and her husband by force to the pond, where they were ducked, thumbs tied to their toes as in many earlier 'trials' of this kind. Both the Osborns drowned, after which a local agitator, a Mr Colley, took a substantial collection of cash from spectators. Colley, who was determined to have stirred up the mob, was tried for murder, to the great displeasure of the people of Tring. A troop of Royal Horse Guards was required to prevent a daring rescue from being staged. Colley was hanged, but too late for the Osborns, victims of a general inclination to lay blame for all misfortunes at the doors of elderly, outspoken and acid-tongued women. 'A Witch and Bitch' indeed. Even in the eighteenth century, it seems there was thought to be no real distinction.

*

The anthropologist Rodney Needham, writing in 1978, defined the witch as 'someone who causes harm to others by mystical means'. Ronald Hutton, in his exhaustive and wide-ranging book *The Witch* (2017), points out that this definition is too limited a reflection of how the word is used in the present day. Hutton argues for a broader definition, including 'one who causes harm by mystical means' as well as 'any person who uses magic' (for any purpose), 'a practitioner of a particular kind of nature-based Pagan religion'; and, interestingly, 'a symbol of independent female authority and resistance to male domination'.

Hutton's definitions resonate for a number of reasons. Firstly, he underscores the fact that, even as other terms lose their gendered meanings – we prefer now to drop the *-ess* suffix and use *actor, poet, priest* as neutral – a witch in 2024 is almost invariably a woman. Historically, this has not always been the case: no fewer than six men were convicted and executed during the hysteria of the infamous Salem Witch Trials, and Hutton does mention various male victims of witch hysteria during its height. Some victims, like Ruth Osborn's husband, were cursed by association – perhaps he should have more successfully controlled his wife. However, these victims were far fewer than their female counterparts by some significant margin. Today, 'witch' in Hutton's fourth sense is often applied misogynistically to women who have, in the eyes of the community, held some authority, and then abused it. When former prime minister Margaret Thatcher died in 2013, 'Ding-Dong! The Witch is Dead' charted at number 2 in the UK. While I, as a child of the coalfields, would be the last person to defend Thatcher's policies, the fact remains that an unpopular male politician would never have been derided in such a way. 'Witch', used in this way, is an insult you can still get away with, its misogyny concealed beneath a superficial layer of plausible deniability. A witch is not only a bad woman, but one who holds some level of power, however darkly wielded. A witch in the twenty-first century is a bitch 'plus'.

While Hutton's first two definitions revolve around, and necessitate, a belief in magic, Hutton points out that 'witch' is now a term of self-definition for many. I've known more than one practising witch in my working life; it's likely that you have, too. With the latest ONS Census data for England and Wales putting the number of those who identify as Wiccan at 13,000, with those who identify as Pagan at 74,000, it isn't really an option not to believe in them. They are real, a now-established part of a society in which hundreds of cultures and religions rub alongside each other in relative comfort. We may not believe Pagans or Wiccans to be capable of magic, but then, they may not either.

Do you believe in witches? You can say yes – you essentially have to say yes – without having to believe in magic, whether foul or fair.

The fact remains, however, that many people still do believe in witches of the magical sort. There are things afoot, they say, that are the preserve of witches, or the strange forces that motivate them; things that are demonic, inexplicable and ineradicable. Thinking back to the unnamed Tyneside man who called Northumbria Police in outrage about the witches stomping about on his roof, we might wonder why on earth it was witches, rather than wildlife or errant teenagers, that were his first thought. Nobody in this day and age bypasses the possibilities of vermin and antisocial behaviour to leap straight to witches – do they?

Well. As with everything, it all depends on your perspective.

*

The perspective from Gibside Hall is not a limited one. After all, that was why it was built where it stands, at the pinnacle of a steep hill commanding spectacular views of the Derwent Valley. From the now-ruined orangery, Mary Eleanor Bowes, the seed from which the Gibside White Lady sprang, could have seen for miles. It's easy to picture her, a pale figure in the darkness, surveying the terrain: Winlaton Mill in the valley far below the estate; the larger village of Winlaton on the hill beyond. Perhaps that's why she's so often seen there still, a stubborn shred of her lingering.

Woodland surrounds and connects the two villages, even today. From the orangery, you can see the bare patches in the woods, marking denes and clearings where the local children play. On one side of the village is Thornley Wood, the woodland of my childhood, frequented in daylight hours by bark-rubbers and dog-walkers. On the other, sloping up towards Winlaton, is Lands Wood, denser and darker – except for the anomaly that is the witches' circle. You can see it clearly from the orangery. Mary Eleanor would have been able to see it, too.

I wonder if she ever knew what it was. The houses Gibside overlooks still displayed physical evidence of belief in witchcraft when, in 1896, the historian William Bourne remarked curiously that 'nearly every door is guarded by a horseshoe'. The witches' circle is only one indication of how deeply the witch threat ran, and still runs, in local lore. But then, although she was raised at Gibside, Mary Eleanor, a cosseted heiress, would not have been exposed to local stories as other girls were. Perhaps she never heard tell of the Winlaton witches. Perhaps, as she walks abroad in her spectral guise, she scoffs at the stories she hears. Ghosts are well and good, but witches? Witches are another story.

The Witches' Circle

In the Derwent Valley, Aiden's grandmother said, you could barely move without bumping into a witch. Cuckoo Nanny was the one everyone knew of, which was odd given how little there apparently was to know about her. Presumably some sort of cunning-woman, no trace of Nanny's one-roomed house remained, but Aiden and his friends could all point out the place where it had stood. Nanny was long gone, but nobody dawdled when passing that field in the dark.

Is a dead witch worse than a living one? Aiden was never sure what the consensus was. He'd heard tell of another local spirit, a child murderer, who stole infants from their beds and drowned them in the river behind The Golden Lion in the valley. She was a witch, people said, but no one knew her name, and Aiden had never heard of a living child taken. Some people said it was her own child she drowned; that the act people allegedly witnessed was little more than a tragic recording inscribed on the earth. She'd been seen often enough, but she never deviated from her path to the river, or lifted her eyes to meet those of the witness. Aiden had no desire to see her himself, but being afraid of a recording struck him as much like being frightened by *The Exorcist:* understandable in the moment, but ultimately rather a waste of energy.

Living witches, though. That was different.

Everybody knew that Winlaton harboured a witches' coven. For most of the year, this fact was presented as entirely normal and unthreatening. Aiden had an aunt who avidly frequented the local Spiritualist church, which seemed not too dissimilar to taking part in Wiccan rituals of a Sunday night. The women called themselves 'white witches' and, while their activities occasioned the odd raised eyebrow, they were not, for the most part, considered a harmful influence. Once or twice, Aiden had glimpsed them at a distance in the woods, gathered around makeshift altars of massed stones, presumably part of what we would now call a Wiccan celebration. Most of the time, these witches were as real and as innocuous as any other gaggle of middle-aged women involved in a group activity.

Most of the time.

A short walk from Winlaton village, there stands a group of oak trees arrayed in a perfect circle. The field in which they stand is an otherwise bare clearing in the middle of a wood; the trees are tall and ancient, their branches intermingling to cast the ground beneath into shadow. For centuries, the copse has been called the witches' circle, a place of curses and hauntings from which children are encouraged to keep away.

And for centuries, naturally, these dire warnings have attracted children like moths to a tantalising flame.

Aiden was eleven or twelve the first time he ventured to the witches' circle on Hallowe'en night. This was a pre-pumpkin era: Aiden and his friends clutched sturdy yellow turnips – what southerners call swedes – painstakingly hollowed out by strong-armed parents. Like many children of the 1990s, Aiden regrets the inevitable slide towards the American jack-o'-lantern; the mottled purple-yellow shell of a turnip with a candle glowing inside is like a severed head, bruised and lit eerily from within. In close procession, the boys snaked through fields with their makeshift lanterns, only a string of yellow lights visible in the dark.

The Circle was their destination, but they never quite reached it. As the copse grew nearer, Aiden's eyes, now adjusted to the pitch darkness, identified a strange glow from within the thicket of trees. A moment later, a hooded figure passed in front of it, and Aiden realised they were looking at a bonfire, and a group of people encircling it. The White Witches had spoken about Samhain and solstice, but never of this: a strange ritual in the darkness, the gathered figures genderless and unidentifiable in white robes, like druids or demon-worshippers. The sort of group who might bring down a curse upon anyone who interrupted them at their work.

Aiden and his friends wasted little time in returning to the street-lit sanctuary of the village, where their parents expected them to be.

The witches' circle, though, became a focus of fascination for Aiden. He and his friends returned the next day in the relative safety of daylight to find the unmistakable aftermath of a bonfire – and a vast slab of stone, set in the middle of the circle of trees. Splashed across the centre of the stone was a blood-red stain, as if it had been used for a sacrifice.

'It's someone's idea of a joke,' said one of Aiden's friends, and everyone murmured uncertain agreement. There was debris lying around the bonfire that spoke of older teens: of course, the witches' circle was the sort of place that would draw sixteen-year-olds playing at being Satanists, especially in the 1990s when this was a bizarrely present preoccupation. Of course, it had probably been pranksters they'd seen in robes the night before, not witches at all.

Still, something about the circle sent shivers coursing through Aiden's body, even though the day was relatively mild. Standing by the stone, he felt impossibly sure of being watched. A friend tried to coax him onto the slab – to lie down upon it like a sacrifice – but he refused. Perhaps the figures they'd seen were only teenage boys, but no teenage boy could have put so weighty a stone where this one lay, entrenched in the earth, covered in moss and that strange dark stain. The ritual might be pretend, but the slab was real.

After that, visiting the Circle on Hallowe'en became a ritual of Aiden's own. As he grew older, he grew braver, too, but something held him back from breaching the Circle itself to confront the figures within it. He told himself it was because, if they were older boys, their reaction to his presence was unlikely to be a positive one. He didn't allow himself to linger on the other, darker possibility – that he'd find this theory to be a false one. That the faces under the hoods would be older ones; grotesque ones; or not faces at all.

The year Aiden was sixteen, he hiked out to the Circle on All Souls' Day with his friends, the way they'd done now for several years. As on previous occasions, the ground was scorched where a bonfire had been; as in previous years, the human detritus of a gathering could be seen littering the grass.

One thing, however, was different. Aiden and his mates had made multiple sallies over the years at moving the huge stone slab – for a laugh, or a dare, or out of morbid curiosity. The slab was immovable, not only by pre-teen boys but also by four now-hefty sixteen-year-olds all working in concert. The slab could only have been brought here by some sort of vehicle, they reasoned. It was beyond human power to lift – which meant that Aiden's throat filled instantly with creeping fear at the realisation that it had gone. There were no tracks in the mud around it, nothing to suggest the presence of a van or crane, or even a rudimentary lever. Where the slab had been, there was only an indentation in the earth, about six feet by two, like a shallow grave.

As the boys looked at each other, the wind picked up out of nowhere, like a warning. For once, they took heed.

After that, Aiden never visited the Circle in the dark again. He didn't want to chance encountering whoever or whatever had moved the enormous slab. But for years afterwards, whenever he went walking in the woods, Aiden kept an eye out for the huge stone and the red stain, just in case the witches had found a new, better place to make their sacrifices.

*

Aiden is a little older than I am, but the witches in his story – the places they're seen, and the places they aren't – are the same ones I grew up with. Local author Paul Brown tells similar tales of the Circle as a fixture of his 1980s childhood, while a novel, *Beyond the Witches' Circle* by Mark Scott, alludes to the local significance of this copse of trees years earlier, in the nineteenth century. I, like Aiden and Paul, remember the eerie slab, and the still-eerier fact of its sudden disappearance; I, too, averted my eyes as I ran past the spot where Cuckoo Nanny supposedly mixed her malevolent potions and glowered at local children out too late. To me, 'witch' has always been a word with several applications; the presence of modern witches is widely acknowledged, but it's clear that Wiccan covens, practising benevolently, aren't really what we're afraid of. What spooks us is the suggestion that something more sinister is still at work beneath.

One of the best-known Derwent Valley witches is seventeenth-century unfortunate Jane Watson, what locals might call a 'proper' witch, from the hanging times. The accusations levelled against Jane were typically bizarre: it was said that she disappeared up a chimney in a streak of fire, having attempted to coax the unwell children of the Cudworth family into eating an apple. The truth, however, seems to relate to Jane's profession as 'a medicer'. One woman, Elizabeth Richardson, claimed that Jane had once healed her of a terrible illness years earlier – but that she had killed the Richardsons' dog in the process. If Jane could cure illness, the suggestion seemed to be that she could also cause it, leaving the Cudworth children in pain and 'bewitched'.

Newcastle, Gateshead and the villages around them suffered more than their fair share of witches in the time of the witchfinders. In 1649, there was thought to be such a proliferation of witch-evil in Newcastle that John Kincaid, then essentially a celebrity 'witch-pricker', was drafted in from Scotland to settle the problem. Kincaid set about pricking the women of Newcastle and Gateshead with his divine bodkin, the idea being that those who didn't bleed were witches, and should be hanged. Of a group of thirty women tried in this way in Newcastle, Kincaid claimed that only three bled. The fact that Kincaid was paid a whopping twenty shillings per proven witch was quite irrelevant – except that, even in the seventeenth century, the local populace didn't always see things that way.

In the end, Kincaid was tried as a fraud and incarcerated, at which point he admitted to his deception. His so-called witches had been no witches at all, and even his contemporaries knew it. Stories like Jane's are remembered in that the accusations levelled against these women are a matter of record, but somehow, the very fact of having lived during such a pitch of witch-fervour protects them. We might believe in the existence of witches, but not of *thirty* witches, at a time when such an accusation was an easy way to deal with an inconvenient woman. On International Women's Day in 2020, the group Witches of Scotland launched a campaign imploring the Scottish government to pardon and memorialise those who were hanged for witchcraft during the purges, a move which quickly gained, and continues to gain, momentum. Is witchcraft real? Possibly. Were these women witches? The general consensus is 'no'. The charges levelled against them were a hateful product of a hysterical time. It was all just – quite literally – a witch-hunt.

But what *is* a witch-hunt? We like to think that, in these enlightened days, nothing like the travesty that was perpetrated in the seventeenth century could ever happen again, but the continued prevalence of the term '*witch-hunt*' says otherwise. The Oxford Dictionary defines a witch-hunt as 'an attempt to find and punish people who hold opinions thought to be unacceptable or dangerous to society'. In this context, the 'witch' is simply the thing we fear. This might be something abstract, like Communism was during the McCarthy era in the United States. At the same time, however, when we call Margaret Thatcher a witch, she becomes emblematic of our social fear of powerful women, unobliging women, and what they might do with their authority. When, in the 1990s, Satanism was proposed with alarming frequency as the reason behind all sorts of social unrest and teenage misbehaviour, the antisocial element of the youth was literally accused of witchcraft, even where the evidence for actual Satanic masses was slim to none. And when the white witches of Winlaton are accepted as benevolent eccentrics by daylight, but suddenly feared capable of blood sacrifice and dark magic on Hallowe'en night, it's not unreasonable to think that some element of Satanic Panic was at play.

We aren't yet too sophisticated for witches, in any sense. The 1735 Witchcraft Act had set to put an end to the witch trials by making it a crime to claim that any person had magical powers or was a witch. The assumption of the bill, unlike in previous Witchcraft Acts, was that witches and magic were not real, and that it was an offence to suggest that they were. However, many people clearly did not share this view. Early practitioners of modern Wicca-type religions would have been committing a criminal act to have identified themselves publicly. Spiritualists and mediums were also at risk. As late as 1944, the Act was used against Jane Rebecca Yorke in east London, who

111

was convicted of 'pretending ... to cause the spirits of deceased persons to be present'.

In 1951, after significant campaigning largely by Spiritualists, the Fraudulent Mediums Act was passed, repealing the Witchcraft Act and making 'express provision for the punishment of persons who fraudulently purport to act as, spiritualistic mediums or to exercise powers of telepathy, clairvoyance or other similar powers' – with 'fraudulent' being a key word. It might have been Spiritualists who drove the change, but as a result of it, the British civil servant and Wiccan Gerald Gardner was emboldened to publish *Witchcraft Today* (1954) and form his own coven, the beginnings of 'Gardnerian Wicca' in the United Kingdom. A new era of witchcraft had been born.

Since the 1950s, the numbers of those identifying as Pagan and Wiccan have increased exponentially. By and large, there is little overt criticism of these beliefs: after all, the Wiccan religion is centred around doing good unto others in hope of receiving good back. If it's magic, it's good magic; and if magic isn't real, then it's no harm, no foul. It's undeniable, though, that many associate Wiccans with the counterculture hippy movement of the 1970s in which paganism flourished; some are vaguely aware of a connection between Wicca and Radical Feminism – Dianic, or goddess-centred, Wicca developed out of the Women's Liberation Movement, with some covens advocating lesbian separatism. The result is that, for some people, the combination of these ideas with the oft-repeated witch's comment that what happens in a coven stays within the coven, sparks a fear not dissimilar to that which drove the purges of the seventeenth century.

In Weelsby Woods near Grimsby, North Lincolnshire, there's another witches' circle which, local rumblings suggest, has stoked still more extreme suspicion than the Winlaton one, with still less foundation. Since the 1950s, Grimbarians claim, the circle has been a meeting place for Wiccan covens. One anonymous source told the *Grimsby Telegraph* in 2020 that 'some witches do slaughter animals for food' in sly confirmation of the rumour that animal sacrifices are regularly made in the circle. Another, equally cloak-and-dagger, said firmly: 'We do not sacrifice animals and what goes on in a witches' circle is private.' One might assume that two competing, equally baseless sources ought to cancel each other out, and yet the possibility of blood sacrifice, cloaked in ritual secrecy, is tantalising enough to win out every time. Interestingly enough, this particular witches' circle was known as a fairy ring until the 1950s. Although a fairy ring is by no means a place of unambiguous good, the rumours of witches are comparatively recent. It's almost as if the repeal of the Witchcraft Act – and the changes in culture and society which took place so rapidly in the mid-twentieth century – set loose both imaginations and tongues. What will become of us if we go about letting people be witches? And what might those witches get up to in our woods, our parks, our communities?

The core of the issue is this: we don't know what these individuals might be concealing under the guise of an innocuous group activity, and that, for whatever reason, frightens us. Their rituals are secret, sacred, not for our eyes, and nobody likes to be excluded in this way – particularly when they are more used to doing the excluding. We know the red stain on the stone slab isn't really blood – but what if it is? Even if our thoroughly modern witches aren't capable of doing magic them-selves, what if the veil is sometimes thin enough for them to pick up on the echoes of someone who could? It's unlikely – we know it's unlikely – but on a dark night, when you stand in the centre of a silent ring of trees, the unlikely suddenly seems very possible indeed.

When I was a child, the stone cairns in the woods used to fill me with such dread that my impulse was always to pull them down, although I never quite under-stood why. Everyone who passed the cairns pulled them down – couldn't chance leaving them alone. Just in case witchcraft – malevolent, uncanny, curse-casting witchcraft – might be real, after all. Just in case the ghost of something gruesome might still be lingering in the woods.

*

This chapter is not about the history of witches. There are plenty of books about that, written by anthropologists and cultural historians whose explorations have led them all over the world over the course of many decades. This chapter is about the *present* of witches, a present which, of course, incorporates and draws from the past but often does so unwittingly or oddly. The witch in the twenty-first century is a funhouse mirror reflection of her Early Modern ancestor, the same general shape and form but with different elements sometimes minimised unexpectedly, or blown up to elephantine proportions.

Generally, we agree that *real* witches – should they actually exist – are bad news. This conviction betrays itself in the blood-sacrifice stories that refuse to die, but also in an interesting tendency to describe a 'bad' ghost as that of a witch. In the previous chapter, we talked about White Ladies and our modern inclination to sympathise with their plights. This is all well and good, but it leaves our more sinister spectres – the murderous mothers, the heart-less hags and the shameless seductresses – kinless. I've speculated that the witch-spirit reported in the Derwent Valley, in her long white gown, is simply an offshoot of the Mary Eleanor Bowes story which elsewhere manifests as the White Lady. This is a ghost whose primary activity is, after all, stealing and drowning babies. This ghost no longer fits into what the White Lady archetype has become. The only option left is to cast her in the guise of the witch.

In European folklore, witches and child murder go together like bacon and eggs. As early as the first century BC, Greek literature contained references to witches who, like Horace's Canidia and Lucan's Erichtho, killed and dismembered children, using their body parts in their

115

potions and rites. Later, the Roman *striga* flew at night in the form of a bird, kidnapping and murdering children and serving as a precursor to the stereotypical witch as we now understand her, a night-flying demoness on a broom, intent on doing harm. The anonymous witch who spoke to the *Grimsby Telegraph* explained that modern witches use brooms to beat away bad energies, but nobody would light upon this as the first obvious connection between the two things. Historically speaking, witches could fly (a concept still evidently alive in the mind of Roof-Witches Man) and they also posed a particular threat to children, an idea that prevailed all throughout the great Witch Trials.

The witch-ghost – the community fear of a once-human entity which was, in life, capable of evil – is not an idea much considered when we think of witches. However, the concept has been surprisingly common for centuries in various forms, and so inconsistent that no modern interpretation could be said to have deviated far from any designated path. There's long been an idea that witches had spirits which could do damage on their own. In some strands of witch-lore, the human body of the witch lay still in her bed at night while her spirit conducted its deadly errands without her, sometimes in animal form. In other traditions, the spirit might be the blackened soul of the witch herself, suggesting that women could be born or become supernatural entities in their own right. Then again, the spirit might be some sort of animus or demon, a dark force separate to the witch herself which used her body as a vessel. In any case, the spirit was absolutely capable of doing no end of damage without the aid of its host body – so why then would it matter if that body had long since turned to dust?

If, in this enlightened age, we're readier to believe in ghosts than in witches, the rise of witch-*ghosts* makes a certain sort of sense. However, the witch spirits of today have a newfound advantage born of our increasing ignorance. According to Ronald Hutton, one of the key characteristics of any type of witch is that it 'can be resisted', something our ancestors believed in earnest. A witch's spirit might be her murder weapon, but murderers can be disarmed. To defend a house against mice, you set up mouse traps. To defend a house against witches, you set up witch traps. It's all very straightforward and, once the witch is ensnared, she can never get free unaided. It's all very straightforward, *if* you know how to set a witch trap. If you don't, you might be in trouble.

*

If you've ever been privy to the inner workings of a building site, it's possible that you've seen a witch trap of your own. A witch might be captured easily enough in a glass bottle, or a sturdy jar, and then buried beneath a house's foundations. Witch traps seem to fall into two categories: repellents and attractants. If we think of witches as a sort of spiritual pest – and our ancestors certainly did – we might think of these two types of traps as equivalent to mosquito repellent spray (which guards a house against potential, but non-specific, invaders) and mouse traps (which capture a pest suspected to be present already, enabling the trapper to dispose of it).

Superstition tends to guide our hand when these arte-facts come to light. Ask any builder: an old shoe up the chimney, or a witch bottle buried by the building's found-ation, is probably there for a reason. It's always best to put it back. There's a sense in many of us that a witch trap is a key to a door we no longer know how to lock again. We don't want to leave the door standing open. You never know what might come through.

Sometimes, though, whether through inattention or foolhardiness, mistakes are made. What happens if we shatter the bottle or uncover the shoe? What if we let a witch's stoppered spirit back out?

Footprints

The coastal town of Berwick-upon-Tweed is technically in England – but only just. It's a hinterland place, histor-ically described as 'of the kingdom, but not in it'. A true Berwick accent is a strange, slippery thing, impossible to place unless you already know where it lives. One moment it's broad Border Scots; then it sidles without warning into something adjacent to Geordie. Helen speaks like this, her voice like a radio tuning in and out of frequency.

A true Berwick accent marks you out. When, in her early thirties, Helen moved to a village in rural Peeblesshire, the distance was trifling – some sixty miles east, and less than ten miles north. But the people of Peeblesshire are Scottish by the grace of God, the majority of them local born and bred. Helen was neither one thing or another – in the kingdom, but not of it – and the unmistakable Berwick burr made this immediately clear to all.

Helen is a primary school teacher. Her university education had taken her as far south as East Anglia and, while her heart belonged in the blustery wilds of the North country, her sensibilities were no-nonsense, cosmopolitan. The romantic in her was drawn to the older houses in Peeblesshire, enticed by their castle-thick walls and steeply pitched roofs. In Peeblesshire, it is possible to buy a beautiful old house on a teacher's salary, and this is what Helen did without compunction. She may have spared a passing thought for energy inefficiency, but she never entertained the threat of the supernatural. Helen didn't believe in that sort of thing.

As it turned out, those in the village had more than enough belief to go around.

It began the day the builders arrived. The village was one of those whose aspect could have belonged to any century, but for the gaudily fronted woollen goods shop which had replaced the traditional spinning mill. Life was a tripartite affair founded upon the school, the pub and the church, so Helen, although not really religious, made it her goal to become a recognised face in all three venues. At first, the mostly elderly congregation had looked at her warily, intrigued by her accent and her heavy, unchurchlike

Doc Martens, but five or six weeks had softened them. They'd become fond of, or at least accustomed to, her presence – or so she thought.

The sight of a half-covered truck outside Helen's house was apparently enough to roll back whatever progress had been made. In previous weeks, various elderly women had paused over coffee in the frigid church hall after Sunday services to share their memories of the house Helen had bought: 'A nice place,' they said. 'Be careful with it.' One of them recalled it from her childhood in the days when an aunt had lived there. The villagers' interest in the house had always seemed benign until the morning the workmen were seen filing in.

Mary, who wore red Wellington boots year-round and never missed a church service, was hovering at the end of Helen's garden by ten. Helen ignored her for as long as she could; the builders were about to take a sledgehammer to the 1970s wood-and-stone surround that had been erected around the fireplace as if in an act of conscious villainy, and her input was needed. The next time Helen glanced out of the window, though, Mary had been joined by two friends. A noise complaint, perhaps? Helen brushed the dust from her sleeves and set off grudgingly down the path.

'Sorry,' was her opener, always a helpful catch-all. 'They won't go on hammering for long. We're just taking it back to the bricks; then it'll be all construction, no destruction.'

The women looked at each other. 'Not knocking out the chimney breast, are you?' Mary asked, as if the answer was important to her.

'No,' Helen assured her, although why this was so important a question was beyond her. She explained about the eyesore of a fireplace. The women looked marginally reassured.

'Need a fire in a house like that,' Mary said. 'If they find anything in the chimney, you make 'em put it back there, you hear? There's stories about that house.'

Her pale eyes bulged encouragingly, an invitation. Helen pointedly did not take it. She wasn't much interested in any stories.

'If they find anything,' she said, 'I'll be sure to let you know.'

The sledgehammering took rather more time than Helen had expected. The new school year was fast approaching and there would be no lesson-planning achieved in this building site, so Helen took her little Nissan Micra over to the next village, which had a library. When she returned, it was to a small crowd in the front garden, larger than the one from the morning. As she drew nearer, she saw that it was anchored around one of the builders. The builder was large and cheery, with a bracing Motherwell accent. He grinned at Helen as she locked the car and hastened near. In his hands – in fact, clutched in his huge right mitt – was what appeared to be a shrunken leather shoe.

'There you are,' he said by way of greeting. 'Thought you'd be interested in this. I've found a few of these in the past.'

He proffered the shoe – definitely a shoe – in her direction. As Helen held out her hand, Mary shot her a warning glance.

'I wouldn't touch it if I were you,' she cautioned. 'That's a witch's shoe, that is. You put it back up the chimney and no harm done.'

The builder's eyes met Helen's conspiratorially. 'Some folk take 'em to museums. They've got some of these in the National Museum of Scotland, I've seen 'em. No good stickin' it back up the flue to rot.'

'No good letting a witch out to roam,' Mary argued. This prompted a murmur of agreement.

'All right,' Helen said diplomatically, 'let's put it back for now. Mary, I promise not to let any witches loose to terrorise the church hall.'

She took the shoe from the builder's hand and walked it firmly back inside, signalling an end to the conversation.

Over the next few days, the builders worked away at the fireplace, carting away the refuse in wheelbarrows until it was time to replaster and rebuild. For whatever reason, Helen put the shoe on the side in the kitchen and left it there. Her first impulse had been to put it on the table, but a stray thought crossed her mind, something her mother had said: never put shoes on a table. That was probably because of witches, too, she thought, wryly. Still, the thing stayed on the side.

The builder who had found it brought up the museum idea several times a day. The shoe was well-preserved, he said, pointing out the visible stitches in the leather and the eyelets for the laces. It also seemed impossibly tiny. What kind of witch could live in a shoe like that? Take it to the museum.

'I will,' Helen told him. For some reason, though, she knew it wasn't really a promise.

When the builders were in the house, generating a comforting hubbub in the living room, the shoe barely crossed her mind. At night, though, it was as if she could feel it, pulsing like Poe's tell-tale heart in the kitchen. Of course it was nothing to do with witches. It was just an old shoe. And yet, what harm would it do to put it back? And what harm could it do if she didn't?

The builders were almost finished when something happened to make Helen's mind up. She'd been baking late one night, unable to sleep. Builders are a hungry lot, and she'd thought to bake a batch of biscuits as a farewell greeting and a thank you. When she'd finished, she left the biscuits out on the side to cool, along with the folded bag of flour and a dish of sugar. She'd put the things away in the morning.

When she came downstairs, a scant six hours later, the sight that greeted her pulled her up short. The bag of flour, which had been neatly folded, was on its end. A cascade of flour had drifted out of it to cover the floor in a dusting of white, like fine snow. In the middle of the patch of flour sat the shoe. And – it was this that made

Helen's chest tighten – next to the shoe, discrete and clear, there was a footprint.

It was uncanny. Helen couldn't think how it was possible. Her immediate impulse was to fall upon it with a sponge and water, as if to eradicate it.

As she scrubbed, thoughts rushed through Helen's head. A mouse, of course, could have knocked both flour and shoe to the floor. But could a mouse have somehow moved the shoe, without scuffing, from its resting place to where she had found it? When she'd lifted the shoe, there had been two clear footprints. She would never forget the way they looked, twin impressions of the past on her kitchen floor.

It couldn't be witches. There was no such thing as witches. Nevertheless, Helen took the shoe hurriedly back into the living room and deposited it on the hearth, as close as possible to the place it had come from. When the builders arrived, they were chuffed with the biscuits, but less so with Helen's insistence that they wall the shoe up again inside the flue, somewhere, somehow. If they knew a safe way to do it?

The big builder sighed, giving her a look of studied disapproval. 'No museum, then?' He took the shoe from her casually, as if it were nothing. 'Aye, all right. 'Course we know *how to do it*. Most people want to put them back, God knows why.'

This, at least, made Helen feel a little better. She knew why.

*

124

June Swann (b. 1929) is a curator generally acknowledged as the world's leading authority on historic shoes. She is also, incidentally, the originator of the field of 'concealed shoes', a subject that had never been extensively studied before she developed an interest in it. Swann's focus on shoes initially sprang from the fact that Northampton, where she worked for thirty years at the Northampton Museum and Art Gallery, was once a shoe-production hub. When Swann retired in 1988, she left behind her an extensive Concealed Shoe Index which is still maintained by the museum to this day, and to which new discoveries are regularly added.

There are many reasons, of course, why concealed shoes might be of interest to a fashion historian. In the first place, stowing a shoe up a chimney is usually a decent means of preserving it, giving us a better understanding of how shoes were made – and mended. A shoe was an expensive item; the vast majority of concealed shoes have been found in working-class dwellings where the cost of the shoe would have far outstripped that of the rest of the outfit. In the area of concealed shoes, though, the interests of the fashion historian and the folklorist inter-twine beautifully. The concealed shoe as a working-class marker helps the historian in that it allows them access, for once, to items worn by ordinary people, rather than by the aristocracy. It helps the folklorist because it tells them that, whatever fear drove people to stow their shoes in fireplaces and foundations, it was not felt as deeply by the upper classes. Most of the shoes that have been found concealed also show signs of extensive wear. For the historian, this provides precious evidence of how shoes were mended, and how long they might be forced to last. For the folklorist, this indicates that a new shoe simply would not do. The shoe must be pressed into shape, reformed in the image of its owner, before it will provide any sort of protection against witches. The shoe, like no other item of clothing, moulds to its wearer, acquiring and then retaining the particular imprint of that person. The shoe of a good person hypothetically contains enough of their moral essence to keep witches away; alternatively, the imprint of their soul upon a well-worn sole might entice the witch's night-borne spirit, then trap her in the toe of the shoe. So it was believed, anyway.

In Helen's story, the protective shoe had clearly done its duty for the better part of two centuries. Part of that duty, Helen pointed out, was to keep the minds of those in the home at rest. A shoe is an incidental sort of witch-trap like a burglar alarm, poised to catch opportunistic intruders creeping in through a keyhole or down a flue. When the shoe was *in situ*, the household felt safe; when Helen made it known that it had been removed, the reaction of the locals suggested a sense of security was no longer warranted. Helen had no real explanation for the floury footsteps in her kitchen, but she's adamant that she would not have considered the possibility of witches had it not been suggested to her. Before she found the shoe – while the shoe was in place – Helen's ignorance protected her. Removing it may not have released a witch, but it certainly brought forth a flood of superstitious unease which, perhaps, is almost as bad.

A woman in Helen's position rarely has to consider the fact that, whatever her advantages over her nineteenth-century contemporary, she doesn't know how to cast a counter-curse, resist black magic, or coax a freed witch back into harness. A witch can be resisted – but only if you know how. Because Helen didn't, the only remedy available to ease her superstitious anxiety was the one that had already been in place – the shoe. She doesn't believe in witches, but she doesn't *dis*believe that something uncanny may be living in her house. If a witch-shoe is an acknowledged talisman against the uncanny, it's a better one than anything else Helen could suggest herself. The footprints, the fear – these, at least, were real. In the circumstances, the best Helen could do was to rely on the expertise of those who, in previous centuries, knew better.

The thing is, while *knowing better* is the sort of thing we might dismiss as belonging to, at the very latest, a steam-powered era, this isn't entirely true. It's instinctive, on some primal level, to destroy any structure we fear a witch has built, even if it's only in our childhood days. If building a cairn summons dark magic, destroying it will surely do the opposite. This is the same sort of logic which dictates that witches dance *widdershins,* or anti-clockwise, when casting their spells, as if moving in opposition to the natural order of things. The two forces cancel one another out. Beyond these instinctive impulses, there is also still a great deal of scrying magic handed down from one generation of teenagers to another, from who-knows-how-distant a starting point. Girls peel oranges at sleepovers and toss the residue over their shoulders, hoping the rind will form the first initial of their future husband's name. They study each other's fingers, sometimes with the helpful aid of a magazine, and read fortunes in the way the fingers taper, or in the shape of the thumb. It doesn't seem much like witchcraft when you're reading aloud from a sugar-pink Summer Special – but it is. We may no longer know a fraction of what our foremothers knew, but some of it still lingers, alongside the human instinct to preserve. If you type the words 'witches' curse' into a search engine, you will happen quite swiftly upon a wikiHow article (with 27 helpful steps!) entitled 'How To Put A Curse On Someone (With Pictures)'. We may not believe it, *really*. But part of us wants to try, just in case.

In some parts of the UK, until incredibly recently, more than just the residue of practical magic lingered. Secreting a shoe up a chimney is a task for an amateur hopeful, but creating a witch bottle requires a significantly more sophisticated practitioner. Charging a witch bottle is targeted magic; usually made of sturdy earthenware, such bottles were meant to capture a particular witch when a person believed themselves afflicted by a curse. Urine, nail clippings and strands of hair from the supposed victim of the witch have all been found inside these containers, alongside rose thorns and iron nails, the better to prick the witch with. Although witch bottles are still regularly found, and often accidentally destroyed, there aren't many people who would know how to create one. It isn't the sort of thing one could search for with much success on Google.

In some places, though, you wouldn't have to.

Witch Bottle

Ron has lived in Wisbech, flush on the border between Cambridgeshire and West Norfolk, for over eighty years. The house he lives in belonged to his parents, and his grandparents before them, and the decor shows it. The carpet in the living room is a dun-coloured paisley affair. The bathroom suite is olive green. And on the bureau, safely at the back of a shelf – *never,* Ron points out, left on the exposed mantelpiece – sits a witch bottle.

In 1944, Ron explains, a witch put a curse on his mother, Ethel. He says this with a smile in his voice, but without apology. His mother, he adds, wasn't a witch herself, but she knew how to deal with them. People still did in those days.

This is a part of the country that has been associated with witches, and other supernatural phenomena, for centuries. Perhaps some of this lies in its landscapes: from the misty Fens to the river-run Broads, this is a watery, liminal place on the eastern edge of England. The notorious witchfinder, Matthew Hopkins, hailed from nearby Ely, and the area was especially plagued with witch trials during his reign of terror.

In the 1640s, those accused of witchcraft could be dealt with by the law. By the 1940s, the afflicted had to take things into their own hands.

With Ethel, it began with an itch – or rather, it was the itching that made her think witchcraft was afoot. For two years prior, since Ethel married a sailor who then swiftly returned to sea, she had been subject to some trouble from the women of the village, all but the oldest and youngest men having gone off to war. Ethel was young and glamorous; a quick and straightforward pregnancy hadn't held her back long from buying black-market lipstick from American soldiers and drawing lines in kohl down her calves to simulate stockings. Sometimes she left Ron with her mother and went to a dance in the next village. The disapproval of many in the village was palpable, but it wasn't until the itching began that she suspected anyone of trying to take action.

Itching, burning, pins and needles – these have been the mark of a witch since the era of the Witch Trials. In Ethel, the sensation began in her feet, then shifted to her fingers. By night, it worsened. There was one particular woman, a decade older than Ethel, who seemed to hold a grudge against her. When this woman looked at her, Ethel said, the itching and burning intensified. As the weeks passed, the pain became worse, until Ethel's toes were painful to walk upon; high heels were certainly out of the question. At first, she put it down to a coincidence. Later, she was sure. Luckily, if it was a curse, she knew how to handle it.

Ron doesn't know where the witch bottle first came from. His grandmother, he suspects, had more than a hand in supplying it. With its round belly and grotesquely bearded face, the bottle is in the same style as similar containers from decades earlier.

'I asked Mum if it wasn't just chilblains,' Ron says, 'but she said this was in high summer, and much worse a pain. Her mother must've believed her.'

You put together a witch bottle, Ron explained, like this: first, find a bottle, or if you haven't one, then make it. You fill it with the essence of yourself: urine, fingernail clippings, hair. Not – importantly! – the essence of the witch, or it will make her stronger. She will already have these things from you, so your object is to stoke up a power that holds more influence than her curse does over the same point of focus (that's you).

You hang the bottle over the fire. You must do this in darkness, in a silent room. In Ethel's case, she took Ron to sleep with his grandmother for the night, just in case he should make a sound that might impede the process.

Your witch bottle will then bring the witch to your door. You will know she is there by the sound of her, the scratching and begging and pleading, the cajoling and, later, crying. If you are strong for long enough, the witch's charm will explode, disintegrate, and become nothing. The spell will be broken, and to keep it that way, you must cork the witch bottle and keep it sealed, forever. This last part is very important. The bottle must be kept, the spell corked inside, *forever.*

After the night of the witch bottle, Ethel said, the pain stopped. The itching receded. She was able to wear her daring shoes again, and the strange pins and needles in her fingers faded away. The woman in the village continued to throw her disapproving glances, but Ethel dismissed them. If she tried anything ever again, Ethel now knew she could handle it.

I asked Ron whether he'd ever been tempted to open the bottle. Ron laughed, then firmly shook his head. He'd often wondered what had really happened, though. Perhaps it had been a case of summer chilblains, or a flare-up of something a doctor could now easily diagnose, but which, in those days, was less explicable. But whatever the truth, Ethel remained adamant to the end of her life that the witch bottle had worked. Over the years that followed, she brought out more than one strange remedy or piece of local wisdom which Ron suspected had roots in witchcraft, or something close to it. She never, to Ron's knowledge, made another witch bottle; but then again, there might only have been the one witch in the village, and Ethel had taken care of her.

Ethel believed in the witch bottle, Ron points out. Maybe that's what made it work. And maybe it isn't.

*

Ron's witch bottle, sitting as it now does like a curio on the bureau in his living room, could easily be dismissed as a relic of a bygone age. After all, the story Ron told me took

132

place in the 1940s, and Ron himself, now eighty, is no longer sure he believes it. And yet, is anything ever really *bygone?* Ron was a child in the '40s, absorbing its scents and sensibilities and the whispers of women who very much believed in witches. That was the era Ron grew up in, and part of it inhabits him like a spirit in a bottle, however changed the world he now lives in. This is the nature of society; and this is why Ron's mother, a twentieth-century housewife with a telephone and, later, a television, still knew how to counter a curse. The knowledge was passed on as part and parcel of the usual pragmatic inheritance: how long to boil an egg; how to replace a lost button; how to stop a curse in its tracks.

Ron still keeps the bottle. When he dies, he says, his children will keep it, too – 'they'd never dare get rid of it'. For as long as the bottle is handled like an unexploded bomb, the age of the counter-curse will never be *bygone.*

Elements of Ethel's story chime with other evidence of spells, protective and reactive, discovered across the centuries. In Hereford City museum, you can see a little wooden doll, or poppet, with cotton arms and legs, wearing a voluminous skirt. When the skirt was found, there was also, in a nineteenth-century hand on a rolled-up scrap of yellowed paper, a spell cast against one Mary Ann Ward, wishing her 'to never rest, nor eat, nor sleep, the rester part of your life'. The presentation, not to mention the flowing hand, suggested a woman-on-woman curse. Meanwhile, in the Museum of Witchcraft and Magic in Boscastle, Cornwall, there is a slingback ladies' shoe of

'80s or '90s provenance, made notable by a needle stuck into the fabric of the toe, a red-orange thread trailing from it. The text says: 'When my lady is out gadding around with Mr Wonderful late at night and I am stuck at home as baby-sitter, who can blame me if I resort to a trick my mother witch taught me – namely how to prick a person's conscience. Yes, it does work.' Shoes, sexual jealousy and sometimes scarlet thread: these measures and counter-measures resonate at the same frequency, from the seventeenth century into the present day.

The *present* of witches in the United Kingdom is, for most of us, very much a just-in-case situation. There isn't, however, a huge amount of evidence to suggest this is a radical shift. As the fate of witchfinder and convicted fraud John Kincaid aptly demonstrates, many people were scep-tical, even in the 1650s, of the idea that witches were roaming the landscape in their hordes. This did not prevent them from concealing shoes up their chimneys as super-natural protection, any more than anything could stop me saluting every magpie I see. Perhaps nothing would happen if I didn't do it, but it only takes a moment. Why chance it? Just in case.

Counter curses have fallen rather more out of fashion, but as is attested by both Ron and wikiHow, there are still situations that might drive us to attempt a little pricking of the thumbs ourselves. When too many things go wrong at once, it's natural to seek a scapegoat to pin it on. The witches of the twenty-first century are the individuals and groups we determine to be the causes of our social ills, and in this, they are little different to the witches of our ancestors. What is a cancel culture call-to-arms, in the end, but the digital equivalent of a (rightful or wrongful) hanging? Our witches will never really leave us. We just want to feel sure that we know how to resist them. In many ways, the retention of this knowledge within our communities is a primary function of our storytelling.

This is, of course, why some of our most terrifying witches are the ones we have no means to contain. The witch spirits of the past could be bottled and booted into silence, but the same isn't true of their enduring spectres, the grim ghosts who re-enact their crimes by night. The malevolent energies attached anecdotally to a witch like Cuckoo Nanny may reflect long-ago panic about old people, strange people, or the mentally unwell, but they live on into the modern age because those fears have not vanished; they have simply become superficially unaccept-able. While a witch's ghost drowns a long-dead baby in the river, there might be a living villain somewhere, committing a similarly horrific act upon someone else's child. However advanced the world may become, we know there's still evil in it: secret societies, such as the Freemasons, still spark terror in some who attribute to them a near-supernatural capacity to control and manipulate society without fear of reprisals. And so, while a coven of Wiccans keeps its secrets close, there will always be some part of us that wonders what they *really* do, and whether it's possible to choose an unusual path without being, in some way, an opposing force in the universe. Nobody likes to see people walking widdershins.

All witch stories are similar, inasmuch as all people are, at heart, living with the same hopes and anxieties. However, it's clear that communities where witch fervour was particularly rife, or particularly enduring, seem to retain its imprint more powerfully on their culture. In Tring, whose strange 'air' meant that witch-hunting prevailed as a mob activity until the late eighteenth century, the memory of that violence still makes itself known – the ghostly din of ancestral attempts to expunge outsiders still echoes through the trees. In Winlaton, meanwhile, the existence of a modern coven stokes the same free-floating fear of deviancy that once drove terror of Cuckoo Nanny and, before that, the trial and execution of multiple cunning women and medicers. The Witches of Winlaton are almost certainly not committing blood sacrifice, but they tread the boundary of acceptability by calling themselves 'witches' in the first place. The copse of trees, the strange cairns, the stone slab – all these features of the local landscape keep witchcraft at the forefront of the mind, meaning it's natural to conflate any malevolent or frightening local spirits with black magic and murder. White Ladies and other benevolent spirits are accepted as part of the landscape, but witches and witch-ghosts are something else – something working against us.

Witches are *within* the community, but they are not *of* it, inasmuch as Berwick is *in* the Kingdom, but not of it. Charlotte, in Peeblesshire, fell into a worryingly similar category when she arrived there with an unfamiliar, unplaceable accent. Naturally, we dislike outsiders; but we are also terrified of being on the outside ourselves. This is why, even if we don't truly believe in witches, it's sometimes easier to keep a witch trap in place, keep the community happy – and signify whose side we're on. Witch traps themselves, after all, perform double duty: they both repel the outsider, and attract the invader, on the off chance that the community has already been infiltrated. It's a multi-lock system, and we are all complicit in it – afraid of what might happen if we cross a witch or, worse, are branded as one.

The earliest written evidence of English spells against witchcraft dates from the tenth century *Lacnunga* and has its roots in a pre-Christian Britain. Witch lore has come to these islands from the Romans, the Saxons and the Norse; it has twined itself through and around an ever-changing religious landscape which it has both borrowed from and disregarded. We have always, in all iterations of our society, been concerned about the presence of witches, deviants and dissidents. After a thousand years, it can be very hard to kick a habit.

※

I noted earlier that the Grimsby witches' circle was once called a fairy ring, which doesn't actually indicate a significant shift in perception. The line between fairies and witches has historically been rather blurred, with iron being posited as a metal that could defend against both, and some witches said to derive their powers from interaction with fairies. Despite their multiplicity of presentation, though, witches remain distinct from fairies in one particular way. Witches might be spirit or flesh; they might fly through the air or move across the earth, though they shrink from water. But unlike fairies, witches don't live *underground.* That strange *middangeard* or Middle Earth, the place between our world and the other side, is not for them. A witch might be incredibly sinister, but what is underground has the potential to be far more so.

Across much of Britain, the ground beneath our feet has been so criss-crossed with mines and tunnels that the thought of a secret kingdom hidden there seems not only fanciful, but impossible. And yet – who of us can say we've never felt the draw of a hole in the ground, whether made by man or by something (someone?) else? When you drop a stone into a mineshaft, it seems to go on and on forever, but that's not possible. It must come out somewhere. But where?

When I asked for ghost stories, strange stories, a surprising number revolved around mineshafts, caves and tunnels, particularly in areas where a job in the guts of the earth had once been the likeliest option for many. This interested me because, set against the clear, continued fascination with witches, the absence of fairies – the original wielders of magic – from the modern mindset is stark. When we think about what lies beneath our feet, our minds no longer stray

138

to the fair folk, but nevertheless, we seem to have replaced them with something.

What, then, do we believe lives underground? Why does it fascinate us? And why do our shuttered coal shafts and tin mines still call to us, decades after the workers downed their tools?

It's time for a journey to the centre of the earth.

Chapter Four

Underground

IN THE SUMMER OF 2022 I went, for the first time, to Naples. Yes, all right, Naples hasn't been part of the same jurisdiction as the United Kingdom since the days of the Roman Empire. But bear with me. This is relevant, I promise – and interesting, if we hope to explore how landscapes and lifestyles help communities birth their own, uniquely nuanced stories.

So: in June '22, I went to Naples. It was my first trip abroad since before the Covid outbreak. I chose Naples less through careful deliberation and more out of a random and urgent desperation to leave the country. Nevertheless, the instinct was a good one. Naples is an ancient city; a vibrant city; a settlement stacked upon thousands of years of history. TripAdvisor told me I'd either love it or hate it. Immediately and unequivocally, I loved it.

For a person who had been confined for several dismal years to Britain's grey shores, the Bay of Naples had one particularly tantalising aspect. From the metropolitan centre of Napoli, sun-drenched Sorrento and picturesque Positano, the turquoise sea ripples out unblemished into the distance, unmissable and unapproachable. From clifftops and scenic overlooks, you can gaze down long- ingly into the water's blue depths, but they're unreachable. The shoreline is too rugged, the descent too steep. Unless you're rich or lucky enough to be staying at a hotel with a private stretch of beach, the sea is to be looked at, perhaps sailed upon, but not bathed in.

Fortunately, mountainous Napoli allows access, by way of compensation, to a yet more compelling subterranean kingdom. You may not be able to access the sea, but gaudy billboards all over the city boast about Naples's catacombs, its crypts and particularly its capacious ancient under- ground reservoirs, which were put to various innovative uses before being finally abandoned in the aftermath of the Second World War. Naples is a notoriously steep city; its quaint funicular railways were built expressly to help citizens ascend to its highest points. If you're curious, though – if you're brave – you can also go down, and down, and down.

In many ways, Naples is a place out of time. Its hilly streets are strung with clotheslines and fairy lights; cats slink serenely, like sure-footed little ghosts, along window ledges significantly narrower than they are. Old men in shirtsleeves smoke from their balconies and, beneath the lofty Cattedrale di San Gennaro, the blood of the city's patron saint is kept in two sacred vials. Three times a year, the long-dried effluvia of this third-century bishop are brought above ground into the sight of the faithful, who pray for it to liquefy, the so-called 'blood miracle'. In 1939, 1940 and 1943, it remained stubbornly dry; Neopolitans did not think it coincidental that Italy, during these years, entered the war in Europe and was subsequently occupied by Nazi forces. In 1980, the blood again failed to liquefy and an earthquake killed almost three thousand Neopolitans. In 2020, the miracle did not occur, and . . . well.

The thing about Naples is this: it may have more layers than a *millefoglie,* but it's still possible to peel apart almost every one and see what lies between. In physical terms, the city peaks at lofty Castel Sant'Elmo and descends through narrow streets right into the subterranean network dug out by the Greeks before the birth of Jesus and put to work by the Romans as aqueducts. In terms of superstition and belief, the many factors at play in Naples are as visible as its disparate physical elements. Geography, climate and culture are inextricably inter-twined here. This is a city where Christian belief was pasted over deep pagan foundations, where the weather can be cataclysmically changeable, and where an under-ground world has been everything from a tomb to a water-tank, supplying the wells of the city before, once drained, it became a haven in which Neapolitans sheltered from Allied bombs. The living and the dead, past and present, are in continual conversation here. In other places, the lines may be blurrier, but we can assume they still run in the same direction.

The second, sunken city of Naples was dug out by hand. From an unprepossessing starting point on the Via dei Tribunali, 136 steps take you forty metres down into this vast space, what the locals call Napoli's womb. Ordinarily, the stairs are dimly lit with electric striplights. I arrived late for a tour, with the result that the lights had been turned off, allowing me the more authentic experience of navigating the concrete steps in pitch blackness. At the bottom of the stairs, you emerge in what appears to be a sort of vast amphitheatre: indeed, it is one. From here, you proceed through cavern after empty cavern, under-ground rooms the size of sports halls, on the walls of which you can still see the crudely carved handholds by which the original excavators descended. No neatly cut stairs for them: on the contrary, they entered the aqueducts through the wells which connected the city above to the water supply, moving like careful wraiths down walls that ran with damp. Beneath them, the water was fast-moving and treacherous; one slip might mean the end. Unfortunately, over the years the system was in operation, there were many more slips than just the one.

This, according to Michael, our effervescent tour guide at the Napoli Sotteranea, is the origin of the mythical *munacielli,* or 'little monks', of Naples. At one point in time, almost every courtyard and grand house in Naples had a well of its own, from which inhabitants could draw water. The *pozzari,* or freelancers, who worked in the water cavities accessed their workplace through these wells – but wells, of course, could also be accessed upwards from the cavities, giving the *pozzari* an easy point of entry to practically any home they chose. One had to be small of stature for this line of work, which entailed squeezing through impossibly narrow passages and tunnels underground. The water caverns were also frigid at all times of year, necessitating hoods and cloaks not dissimilar to those a monk might wear. So, when a *pozzaro* was glimpsed entering or exiting a well, he might easily be mistaken for – that's it – a little monk. I came home from Naples with a *munaciello* figurine. About an inch high, he lives in a matchbox and is, according to Michael, a good luck charm. The little monks are among the most enduring and notorious inhabitants of Naples, but, unlike my pocket-sized friend, they don't always bring good luck. On the contrary, these are complex and enigmatic creatures – by some accounts spirits that once were human, and by others, something stranger and perhaps more sinister. Like the sea or the smouldering volcanoes of Campania, the *munacielli* must be treated with the respect they deserve. When you are kind to them, they offer you kindness in return, but if you aren't? That way, trouble lies.

Nothing in Naples, however, is what it appears.

There's another story behind the *munaciello.* In this one, the creature is a single spirit, that of a deformed child raised in a fifteenth-century nunnery. His parents, a labourer and an heiress, were star-crossed lovers; the doomed romance ended in the murder of the father and the confinement of the mother to a convent. The child concealed his overly large head in either a black cowl (which brought bad luck) or a red one (which brought good). Unfortunately for all concerned, the red cowl made only very infrequent appearances, and the child, having become a much-feared bad omen, came to an untimely and unexplained demise.

Michael's opinion is that this story is just that: a story, told to frighten children at bedtime. It's much more logical, he said, to assume what people saw were real workers clambering in and out of the water system, sometimes pilfering gold from rich families who'd wronged them, sometimes leaving food for those who were struggling. The simplest explanations, Michael declared, were usually the best. Whatever their true origin, the 'little monks' of Naples represent a leap from fact to folklore so beautifully clear that it serves as a fascinating roadmap for how, in other places where the layers of history are more messily stuck together, similar journeys may have been made.

Michael had no explanation, however, for the proliferation of *munacielli* sightings still recorded annually in Naples. Perhaps the *pozzari* who gave rise to the Little Monk stories were real – but what of the *munacielli* still supposedly roaming the city to this day?

Michael, with Campanian insouciance, only smiled and shrugged in response to this question. 'They're real too,' he said. 'Why not? I've seen them.'

Il Munaciello

The *munacielli*, Michael says, are rife in the older parts of Naples. More than once, he has seen the hooded figures slipping past like shadows in the dark; near Piazza Garibaldi, their indistinct shapes might be glimpsed from the corner of an eye, lingering in doorways and ducking into alleyways. They want you to follow them, Michael says (although personally, he would never commit such a foolish act). The *munaciello*, in its red-cowled state, can bring great good fortune, but equally its black-hooded form is a dispenser of nightmares – and the black and the red are, in darkness, indistinguishable.

Besides, Michael says, even a *munaciello* fortune might ultimately spell disaster. The creatures are irascible, unpredictable, and demand total silence from those they choose to favour. The money they bring you is tainted, and it comes with conditions.

The Via dei Tribunali is the artery at the core of central Naples. In the Roman city of Neapolis, it was the *Decumanus Maggiore*, the main street running east to west across the town. Beneath it, the route of the Sotteranea, the city's underground world, runs in parallel. Today, there are no fewer than eighteen churches along the three-quarters-of-a-mile length of the street, including the spectacular Duomo di Napoli. It's almost as if the inhabitants of the Via dei Tribunali, throughout its thousands of years of history, have often found themselves in need of spiritual protection.

In this part of Naples, the prevalence of the *munacielli* has long been widely accepted. As early as the sixteenth century, the *Pragmatica de Locto et Conduco* – a hefty tome intended to regulate housing law in the city – contained a proviso that left tenants free to leave a house, rent unpaid, should it be plagued by a *munaciello*. Of course, the presence of the creature in your home *could* bring wealth and fame to its inhabitants, but for many, the risks outweighed the potential rewards. Once a house became known to be a *munacielli* den, the likelihood of its owner making a success of it as a rental opportunity would only decrease. Rents fell; landlords became desperate. Of course, there will always be those so desperate themselves that a cut-price rental is impossible to turn down, even if it comes with a haunting.

There is one house on the Via dei Tribunali – locals can still point it out today – which was once so plagued by a *munaciello* that tenant after tenant fled from it until, eventually, a student took it on. He was not a Neapolitan, and the whispers of his neighbours struck him as nonsense. All he knew was that the house was grander than anything he should feasibly have been able to inhabit on his meagre income, and that the landlord had appeared unwilling to give any explanation for the minuscule fees he asked. It struck the student that some sort of odd superstition had turned the locals' brains – but it was he, after all, who was the beneficiary of it. There was no such thing, to his mind, as a haunting. There were only good deals, and those who could ill afford to turn them down.

The disturbances began again almost as soon as the student took possession. At first, they manifested as sounds: scuffs and bangs in the night. Then, things began to go missing. The student would find his socks had vanished, or the food he'd laid out in the evening to take out with him the following day. The student had seen no evidence of the perpetrator – but he began to suspect he knew what was behind both the nocturnal occurrences and the local superstition. What was an old house without mice in its walls?

He bought a cat.

The cat, however, did not put an end to the noises. On the contrary, its presence seemed to exacerbate matters. One night, a shelf laden with china became detached from its moorings and fell from the kitchen wall to the tiled floor, sending shards of crockery spiralling in all directions. Had the student mentioned this to any of his friends or neighbours, they would no doubt have urged him to flee the premises, but the student was becoming stubborn now. He put the shelf back up, telling himself that nails could bend and plaster could crumble.

The next night, he was awoken by the ringing of a handbell in his living room, first desultory, and then increasingly urgent. Infuriated, the student began to wonder whether the neighbours' stories were, in fact, a reaction to a stranger in their midst – an attempt to drive him out of his home. He pulled the covers over his head and felt sure there'd be a window standing open when he woke in the morning, through which some local boy had slipped, intent on causing mischief.

In the event, sleep was not to be. The bell ringers, apparently unwilling to concede defeat, progressed to hurling pans, pots, lids – anything they could find – in the direction of the student's bedroom door. Eventually, the door creaked open and the student, unwillingly, rolled over, expecting to be confronted with a recalcitrant child.

According to Neapolitans, what he saw instead was the *munaciello,* irate at having been ignored for so long. Bleary-eyed and exhausted from many nights of disturbed sleep, the student decided he must be dreaming. When the creature warned him to tell nobody of what he had seen, promising to reward him if he obeyed, the student simply shrugged and went back to sleep.

The disturbances in the house, Michael says, immediately stopped. Neighbours were baffled to see the student so nonchalantly come and go, apparently undeterred by whatever else lived inside his house. Had he made a bargain with the *munaciello?* As the years passed, and the student became an increasingly rich and successful man, they were sure of it. The *munaciello* had smiled upon him in return for his silence.

The student died a very rich man, and it was muttered in the area that perhaps, when he died, it would be in the best interests of somebody to take over the lease on the lucky-unlucky house. In the event, though, nobody dared, and for years it stood empty, the presence of the *munaciello* inside more thoroughly confirmed than ever. The student might have chosen to dice with the Devil, but he was a foreigner. No Neapolitan would be so foolhardy.

*

The *munaciello* of the Via dei Tribulani is an interesting story in that, really, it isn't at all about what the student saw, or did, or believed. On the contrary, it's a story about how those around him interpreted his actions through the lens of their own superstition. It is, of course, entirely possible that the house was simply built on unstable foundations and riddled with mice, which bothered Neapolitans (convinced they were being haunted) but didn't faze the student, who didn't believe in *munacielli* but *did* believe in building his fortune on the foundation of obscenely cheap rent.

Still, for those who believed in the *munaciello,* nothing the student did could have convinced them it did not exist. If the student had suffered misfortune, it would have been the creature's fault; because he stayed and prospered, this, too, must be somehow the responsibility of the *munaciello.* In her 1884 book *Di lei Il ventre di Napoli,* Matilde Serao asserted that there stood a spectacularly beautiful building in Salita Santa Teresa, central Naples, which was impossible to let due to its reputation of being 'inhabited by spirits'. Today, Michael says, there are still many houses in this area where rents are lowered and prospects dimmed because of the belief that spirits lurk in dark corners.

Another interesting element about the *munacielli* is that, while they are ubiquitous in the Bay of Naples, they also share characteristics with other underground creatures, not only across southern Italy but also in the wider European context. The idea of the creature as a disturber of sleep is echoed in the form of the *monachicchio*, gnome-like beings who plague the Basilicata region of Italy, sitting on and pinching sleepers in their beds. *Monachicchi*, like *munacielli*, translates literally to 'little monks', but, unlike their Neapolitan counterparts, the *monachicchi* always wear red hats which seem to be the source of their power. If the hats are stolen, the creatures are rendered helpless.

This curious red hat idea is also found in Salento, where the *Scazzamurrieddhru* protects young women and pets, but also has a penchant for crushing the chests of sleepers. If the inhabitants of a house are kind to it, it will be kind to them; if not, they must beware. In Romagna, the *Mazapegol* retains the red cap of its southern kin, but the more prosperous elements of the legend seem to have been lost and the creature is closer to a nightmare spirit. Many stories about its exploits seem to describe what today would be interpreted as sleep paralysis, and, interestingly, the association with the underground realm is largely absent.

*

Anyone familiar with the rural lore of the Border counties between England and Scotland might recognise a strange connection between these cryptic Italian beings and a creature rumoured to plague the numerous castles and bastle houses which, in the brutal days of the Border Reivers, from the late thirteenth to early seventeenth century, were the site of much conflict. The redcap, or powrie, is a goblin-like entity whose cap acquires its scarlet colour not by natural means, but through being soaked in the blood of the creature's victims – usually travellers who stray into redcap territory. Unlike the *munaciello*, the redcap is, in most instances, unequivocally ill-intentioned: should the blood on a redcap's cap go dry, the creature will perish, making regular kills imperative. Occasionally, though, we find a more ambiguous example, such as the redcap of Grantully Castle in Perthshire, the sight of whom brings good fortune to the beholder. Goblin-like beings of this sort run the gamut from the villainous to the bene-volent, with the *munaciello* being perhaps a little more vindictive than the English brownie, and the redcap usually more in the realm of the Romagnan *mazapegol*, its scarlet-hatted counterpart. The origin of the red hats themselves is unclear, although the redcaps' explanation is simple enough. Throughout Europe, perhaps the only other obvious comparison to be made is with the Irish *far darrig*, or red man, a practical joker not unlike the leprechaun.

Of course, for most people in the Borderlands, the redcap is now nothing more than a children's story. Unlike the *munaciello*, the fear of it can no longer drive down property value, or cast a pall of suspicion over a person's sudden fortune. This is not to say, however, that relatives of the redcap do not continue to haunt the Borderlands. It's notable that the redcaps themselves were castle-dwellers, never fond of cramped holes or chalky cellars. Above ground, there's light and life enough that the old stories have, for the most part, been swept away. Below ground, though? Well.

In many parts of the Borderlands, the underground world – caves and coal mines; pits and pick faces – has long been as present in daily life as it is in Naples. The things that live here, like the *munaciello* but unlike their redcap cousins, have been protected from the momentum of modern life. Underground, there's a place in which their memory still thrives, alongside the cultures of communities shaped by their mining history.

Miners have always been a superstitious lot. They have good reason to be. For hundreds of years, significant tranches of northern England, Cornwall and Wales were identified by their mining culture; many of these places are now defined by the loss of it. They are *post*-industrial. Like Winlaton Mill and some of the other towns described in Chapter One, they are 'former' mining towns. In some ways, this naming convention seems bizarre: the last mines in Britain closed, with very few exceptions, in the 1980s. The only miners still living in these areas are long retired. And yet, in other ways, the continued association makes sense. While mining may have ceased, the presence of the mines themselves has not. You can fill in a pit and build a country park on top of it, but the seams cut into and out of the earth will always remain – as will the scars cut into the culture of a place by the miners who tunnelled beneath it. Sometimes, the evidence is found in language: dialects like County Durham's 'pitmatic' show the influence of miners' talk on an already-distinct local tongue. Sometimes, it's in the way communities were built and rebuilt to accommodate weak places in the earth, avoiding a spot where a pit once fell in and killed hundreds. And sometimes, it's in superstitions that the memory of mining is most strongly felt. The miners might all have long abandoned their underground tasks, but their strange underground companions received no similar edicts from Thatcher to come to the surface and join the modern world. Those who worked alongside the human toilers, according to some, have never left the mines.

These supernatural beings in the mines go by many names. The most obvious cousin of the *munaciello* and his red cowl is the bluecap, a thing more fairy than goblin, whose glowing blue flame guides respectful workers to rich deposits of ore or away from potential cave-ins. (I'm sure you can imagine what happens to the disrespectful.) Similar creatures elsewhere go by many names, but all perform similar functions: on a good day, the being might not only direct weary miners to a good seam, but may also help to work it. Their telltale glow could indicate the presence of good fortune – or bad.

Other pseudonyms for bluecap include *kobold* or *coblynau,* both words directly related to English 'goblin'.

The German *kobold,* in fact, gave its name to the mineral cobalt due to a medieval belief that it was responsible for the poisonous qualities of the ores, like cobaltite and smaltite, that were mined. This sort of creature is now best known by its Cornish name, not only because Cornwall was so replete with mines, but because so many of its miners made the long journey across the Atlantic to the United States, taking their folklore with them. Cornish words made their way into the local language, and thus, almost incidentally, into literature which circulated around the world. Nothing is set in stone: an old idea can readily take on a newer name, the better to fit under the skin of a new society. The Cornish called these creatures knockers; their Pennsylvanian descendants added the prefix Tommy. Stephen King made the word resonate around the globe in the third-bestselling book of the 1980s – and, although his lurid, drug-fuelled interpretation of the creatures is more Lovecraft than folk legend, it's done more than any other to cement them in popular culture.

Tommyknockers it is.

*

When Cornish miners began relocating in their droves to California in the first half of the nineteenth century, it was their expertise the Americans wanted. The skills involved in mining tin – uniquely found, within the UK, in Cornwall – are readily transferable to gold-mining, and many a Cousin Jack had his boat fare paid by a

Forty-Niner keen to bolster the knowledge and experience of his team. What the Americans did not anticipate, however, was that pragmatic skills were not all the Cornish would bring with them. The miners knew how to safely wield a pick, how to tap a vein. They knew the importance of communication, preparation and anticipation in making sure all those who entered a pit also made it out again. But they also knew that there were more things in the mines than were dreamed of in the Americans' philosophy. A pit without knockers is a pit without fortune. The Cornish refused to be budged on this point; eventually, the Americans conceded it. No Cousin Jack would enter a mine without being assured of the presence of knockers inside it, protecting the workers from harm. Those who believed in the knockers paid attention to the creaks and rappings they made, which signified imminent danger or collapse. Those who refused to heed the knockers' warnings, the Cornish said, could expect an unhappy demise.

By the time the mining industry of El Dorado County, California, came to an abrupt and rather ignominious end in 1956, the miners were well trained in the need to respect their mysterious colleagues. The manager of one of the oldest and largest mines in the area was petitioned to formally release the mine's tommyknockers from employment so that they could find work elsewhere within the Californian mining system. After all, more than one mine had been abandoned after repeated knockings and collapses led the workers to believe the knockers there had been angered: who knew what might happen if the creatures were locked up in the pit without warning, after years of being heeded as respected colleagues?

A scientific mind might argue that the knockers' signatures – taps and creaks which inevitably preceded disaster; an eerie blue glow in the darkness – were caused by gas and natural subsidence, the inevitable result of messing about underground. The manager didn't care to take the chance. He formally released the tommyknockers, and the miners were able to go on with their lives undogged by the fear of having crossed a creature of unknown temperament and influence.

The same could not be said, however, of many of their counterparts in the United Kingdom, where the career of the knockers first began. Across the country, mines of all stripes – tin, coal, copper – limped along through the latter part of the twentieth century, the blue light of the knocker legend growing vaguer and more indistinct until, in some areas, it flickered out almost entirely. Against a backdrop of Band-Aid and Betamax, to say nothing of years of pitched battle between trade unions and the government, the smallest inhabitants of Britain's mines became somewhat lost within the big picture. Nobody petitioned for their fair treatment; after all, if human workers couldn't expect as much, what hope had a bluecap or a *coblynau*? The mines were shuttered, and with them the hopes of countless communities.

The knockers, however, were still there.

Tommyknockers

Ritchie's house was built upon a pit. This is not, in itself, unusual; Northumberland and County Durham are so honeycombed with disused shafts and tunnels that many a recent housing development has arisen upon reclaimed mining ground, stacked on the skeleton of industry. But in Ritchie's house, there was still more than a flicker of flesh on the old bones; and where others might dismiss nocturnal noises as the ordinary sounds a house makes, Ritchie knows better. He knows there's something still living in the pit, years after the last man left it. After all, he spent ten years underground himself. You can take the miner out of the mine, but never the mine out of the miner.

All houses make noises. When you live somewhere, you learn its tics: the gurgling sounds air makes in the pipes when the boiler's turned off and the nervous habit of the floorboards on the landing which creak as they settle. When people hear of tapping and groaning in a house, Ritchie thinks, this is what they imagine – the ordinary sounds with which any reasonable person will become, in time, acquainted. These are not the sorts of sounds Ritchie's house made.

The first time he heard the night noises, Ritchie says, his initial assumption was that he was being burgled. The door to Ritchie's bedroom was directly opposite the top of the stairs, and up those stairs, or so it seemed, footsteps were coming. No tiptoeing, careful steps here, as you might expect from an intruder in a dark house, but the heavy, booted stomps of, Ritchie thought, at least two men. He sat bolt upright in bed, breathing heavily, the sweat pooling cold between his shoulder blades. He was alone in the house. Should he even attempt to confront two such reckless men? His phone was charging on the bedside table. Perhaps he should simply call the police?

The footsteps were growing louder, heavier, closer. Ritchie reached for his phone. It was while he was dialling 999 that they reached the landing and then – immediately, impossibly – fell silent.

Ritchie's heart thundered in his throat. He clutched the phone tightly in his hand and strained to hear over the rushing of the blood in his ears. How could such footsteps simply disappear? But there was no creaking of floor-boards; no rustle, however infinitesimal, of clothing. Whoever had mounted the stairs was either stock-still and breathless on the landing, or—

Or he wasn't.

Ritchie sat, unmoving, in bed until dawn crept in through the curtains, at which point he felt finally able to get up and open the door. There was, of course, nobody on the landing. The runner on the stairs was undisturbed. Whatever he had heard had vanished as if it had never been.

That was the first time.

Over the course of his first year in the house, Ritchie heard the footsteps on the stairs perhaps five or six times. Each time, the sound yanked him abruptly from sleep; sometimes the footsteps were accompanied by odd, metallic thuds, as of a hammer on metal. Invariably, when they reached the landing, the sounds instantly ceased. Ritchie, a stocky, popular chap in his mid-thirties with something of a reputation as a hard man, said nothing to anybody until, one evening in The Rose and Crown, his girlfriend Ailsa noticed he looked harried and tired.

'Have I been keeping you up?' she teased.

Ritchie swallowed, then said that, on the contrary, if she'd been in his bed the night before, it probably wouldn't have happened.

'It?' she asked, and Ritchie knew he was committed. He told her the story. He expected her to be disbelieving, at best; at worst, concerned for his mental state. What he didn't expect was the smile that spread across her face, somewhere between recognition and outright delight.

'Ritchie,' she said, thrilled, 'you've got tommyknockers!'

Ritchie's brow furrowed. 'I've got what?' He'd never heard the word before.

'Tommyknockers,' Ailsa repeated. 'Didn't you work down Ellington Pit? How've you never heard of knockers? My dad could talk your ear off about them.'

Ritchie was lost. He hadn't come from a mining family. He'd taken the job at Ellington Pit in 1999 because it paid better than the bricklaying he'd done previously, and to which he had now returned. By that time, the pit was swiftly nearing its final closure and its routines and rituals, conducted three miles beneath the North Sea, already felt like relics of a bygone age. At Ellington Colliery in the early 2000s, the miners no longer spoke of knockers. As

Ailsa described them, though – the hammering, the tramping boots, the blue glow in the darkness – Ritchie realised this didn't mean there weren't any there. In fact, all unknowingly, he'd seen them.

*

It was on a Sunday. Ritchie couldn't be sure of the year, but he knew it was a Sunday because Sunday overtime paid double, which was why he and his mate Dodd felt it justified hard graft on a hangover. A conveyor belt at the colliery had become blocked by a fall of coal. Ritchie and Dodd, buoyed by the promise of a fatter than usual pay-packet, volunteered to unblock it.

Once upon a time, a seam like Ellington would have been mined every day of the year save Christmas, but this was the twenty-first century. While the task of coal-mining itself remained inescapably Victorian, the miners had thoroughly modern health and safety, and they didn't work Sundays. Ritchie hadn't bargained on how much more eerie the pit would seem once devoid of anyone but himself and Dodd, their cap lamps the only defence against total darkness. Still, the more hours they spent in the hole, the bigger the pay packet. Neither Ritchie nor Dodd had any intention of doing the job at speed, however cavernous and quiet their underground world suddenly seemed.

The task itself was simple enough. The two men, upon arriving at their workstation, decided to reward themselves with an hour's break, after which they reluctantly took up their long-handled shovels and began shifting the blockage. The motor itself was trapped; once it was free, the coal could be carried away by the conveyor belt. To this end, the miners worked – not too quickly – to deposit the coal onto the belt itself, away from the motor. Once it was up and running, the belt would carry them, too, out of the mine and back to the safety of a Sunday afternoon on the north coast.

The benefit of simple, mindless tasks is that they do at least provide equally straightforward rewards. When, after some hours of toil, Dodd tried the button, the belt whirred comfortingly to life. The blockage was cleared; the belt worked. Dodd threw Ritchie a knowing glance.

'Shall we have a kip? We can get another hour's pay out of this at least.'

Ritchie laughed, in total agreement with this plan, and the two men turned off their cap lamps, throwing the pit into total darkness. The belt whirred on, providing a sort of comforting white noise. With arms crossed and chin on chest, it took Ritchie mere minutes to fall asleep.

Asked to imagine complete darkness, most people will picture a curtained room; a starless night; the cupboard under the stairs where they liked to hide as a child. Above ground, though, no darkness is complete. The darkest night contains a memory of daytime. A pit doesn't know what daytime is. When Ritchie opened his eyes, it was to perfect, unleavened blackness. The conveyor belt was still whirring, and something – someone – was coming towards him unseen, their heavy tread echoing in the enclosed space.

Ritchie's stomach clenched. He knew at once that Dodd, too, was awake, but his tongue seemed stuck in his mouth. He couldn't move. The footsteps moved closer, and Ritchie thought wildly that someone must have got trapped down here; some lone worker – not allowed – if he could only make his arms work, he could snap on his cap light and sort it out once and for all—

It was at this moment that, as if it had heard his thoughts, the light appeared.

Dodd inhaled sharply, a ragged catch of breath. Ritchie couldn't make a sound. They simply sat there in the pitch blackness, listening to the footsteps and watching the light. Cap lights were yellow, but this light, Ritchie said, was pale blue and flickering. The belt continued to chunter away from them, out of the mine, and meanwhile the blue light drifted steadily in the opposite direction, drawing nearer and nearer.

'Shit!' That was Dodd. His cap-light flicked on, and Ritchie made a sound he'd later deny ever having uttered, immediately closing his eyes as if to preserve his ignorance. The footsteps, though, abruptly stopped. When Ritchie dared to open his eyes again, there was no sign of the light – no sign of anything. They were alone in the mine. The belt kept whirring, its cargo long since transported to the surface.

'Come on,' Dodd said, in a voice Ritchie barely recognised. 'Let's get out of here.'

Ritchie didn't need telling twice – and he never worked on a Sunday again. There wasn't enough overtime in the world.

Ritchie didn't tell this story to Ailsa. He didn't tell it to anyone. It had so shaken him that he'd been almost grateful when, just a few years later, the colliery closed. Ritchie reasoned that a place that had functioned as a mine for almost a hundred years couldn't possibly help containing a ghost or two, but he had no desire to come face to face with them.

Ailsa's father, long since retired, believed in pit ghosts, too, but what Ritchie had seen and heard matched far more closely with what the older men called *knockers*. Some people thought knockers in a house were an omen of death – that the creatures only came above ground to issue dire warnings. Ritchie didn't know if he believed that. Nobody had died, and they'd have to come above ground now, wouldn't they, if they wanted to be heard? It made sense, but it didn't mean Ritchie wanted to be the one to hear them. Ghosts, goblins – it was all one to him.

He sold the house, taking care not to advertise the fact of its additional inhabitants. He bought a flat, having ascertained it had no connection with, proximity to, or attachment to a pit. Knockers, he thought, may have the right to exist, as long as they stay as far away from Ritchie as possible. His mining days were over.

*

Ritchie's story is only one of several I gleaned from former miners, many of which shared similar elements. Ritchie's was the most involved; moreover, it was told to me in person, but when I put out a request online for mining tales, I encountered no shortage of pitmen keen to share their memories of glowing lights and mysterious footsteps, far below the ground. The independent author Brian Long has compiled two collections of miners' tales, primarily sourced from forums and private online groups: *Tales from the Deep* and *Presence in the Pit,* both of which make for an interesting perusal. Brian, himself a retired miner, writes: 'Some say that a spirit never leaves the pit, carrying on with the job they left behind; some say they come back to check on their friends . . . What we nearly all agree is that mines are an eerie place to work.'

It isn't difficult to understand why. My ancestors were miners for generations. One family photo is marked by little crosses to show which of the brothers in it were lost to pit collapse. As a child, I enjoyed being thrilled and terrified by the drift mine at Beamish Open Air Museum, County Durham, where visitors are warned:

- The minimum head height in the mine drops to 4 feet 6 inches (140 cm). Anyone above this height must be able to stoop during the tour.
- The surface, underfoot, is made up of gravel and is uneven. There is also standing water on the ground.
- Visitors are free to leave the tour, at any point, and return to the surface.

Those who actually worked down the mine when it was a functioning colliery, of course, were not afforded the same privilege.

The slate mine at Blaenau Ffestiniog in Gwynedd, Wales, is another site of industry-turned-tourist attraction where the shocking subterranean reality of mining can be personally experienced. My partner and I descended, with a guide, into the depths in a cage that rattled alarmingly as it moved. Once underground, our guide explained how the 'Miners' Hymn' was once sung to share the news of a death or injury: the song would spread from chamber to chamber until it reached the surface. She then turned out the lights, and played the hymn. Rarely have I felt such goosebumps. It isn't difficult to see why, working under such circumstances, miners might have lived with the perpetual expectation of seeing spectres in their midst.

But were they really there? One ex-miner, David, was sure that they were. Not just occasionally, but often.

Headcount

When a colliery shift was finished, it was possible to walk, if you absolutely had to, back to the cage that waited at the bottom of the shaft to carry workers back up to the surface. Possible – but, as it would have required half an hour's brisk motion, it wasn't thought ideal by the miners who'd just finished an arduous eight-hour shift below ground. Better to catch the train which could carry six men – just about – the distance to the shaft, and from there to be loaded into the cage and lifted towards daylight.

There were almost always six men in the train, David said. Even if there were only four men on shift, and four men in the cage, more likely than not there'd be six men in the train.

'You weren't supposed to notice,' he explained. 'You weren't supposed to point it out. It was as if something terrible would happen if you did.'

The first time, of course, David did. Exhausted, coated thickly in soot, he could barely keep his eyes open as the train rattled towards its destination. Pinned on both sides by the strong shoulders of other tired men, he felt his head nodding as salvation and the shaft drew near. The train was full; full to capacity, its inhabitants crammed together like sardines.

When it finally rattled to a halt, the miners were jostled awake. Yawning, David waited for his neighbour to exit, and then followed him out of the train. Fighting sleep, he stumbled towards the cage and settled himself inside. Only when the motor began to whir did he register, suddenly, how much more room he now had: no heavy chest crushed against his back, nobody breathing on the back of his neck. He roused himself and addressed the operator.

'What about the others?' he asked. 'Wait for the others!'

The operator smiled, as if he'd heard this before. He had, of course. Nothing is more predictable than life down a mine.

'This is the lot,' he said. 'Four of you. See?'

David scanned the darkness. There was nobody else waiting – nobody struggling to exit the train. There were four men in the cage; there had been, quite distinctly, six men in the train.

'Apparently,' David explained, 'you never get over your desperation not to miss it.'

This is a supposition borne out by other stories, from other mines: from Morpeth to Abercynon, there were often too many men in the train. Some people just can't clock off – however hard they try.

*

As these stories show, folklore isn't something which, like a child, is born, establishes itself, develops – and then dies. It's cyclical, self-perpetuating. The little monks of Napoli developed organically as a result of the city's shape and its industries; like the knockers, they're still there, even now the human workers have long since departed. Further abroad, too, the seeds of an ancient idea can be sown in new soil and produce their own hybrid varieties, just as the Cornish took their mining spirits to the United States and, in a brave new world, transformed them into their American cousins, the tommyknockers. The original mine-dwellers of the British Isles – the knockers, bluecaps, *coblynau* – were fairy kin, inhabitants of the ancestral underground realm of the Fair Folk. In the United States, removed from this context, they are more usually imagined to be of once-human stock, the ghosts of long-dead miners still protecting their descendants. A tommyknocker may once have been a bluecap, but the reverse is not true; as the Norse god Odin says of his offshoot Mr Wednesday in Neil Gaiman's *American Gods,* 'He was me, yes. But I am not him.' The context reinvents the creature, not merely keeping it alive but endlessly multiplying its forms.

For Ritchie, too, the concept of a ghost settled far less uneasily in his mind than that of a goblin or fairy. A child of the 1970s, he was raised to think of fairies as twee little sprites, like Tinkerbell, not as will-o'-the-wisps, child abductors or spellbinders. But the notion of knockers, a local superstition regifted to him from within his own community, allowed him to reframe and recategorise his own experience. Ritchie still conceives of knockers as something more akin to a spirit, but what, after all, is the active difference between the thunderous, disembodied footsteps of fairies, and those of ghosts? Is there one? Does it matter? Across distances both physical and temporal, the same ideas and interactions constantly recur and are interpreted according to the knowledge and cultural context of the experiencer. When thirteenth-century Scottish laird, Thomas the Rhymer, was spirited away for seven years and shown the marvels of the universe, the culprit was the Queen of Elfland. Similar episodes of lost time, abduction and hallucinations in the last century have been attributed to extraterrestrial beings. The effect is the same.

We no longer default to fairies when we think of what lives underground, but for as long as there's an underground world, it seems, we still want to picture something in it. In some communities, such as the Navajo and

Pueblo tribes in the south-western United States, the earth is conceived of as a womb from which all life sprang, and returning to it is a consummation devoutly to be wished. In much of the West, however, to descend below the surface of the earth is to alienate oneself increasingly with every metre travelled from a sky-bound God. It follows that, if you must creep closer to the Devil, you should not be surprised to come face-to-face with his associates.

In the twenty-first century, there is one particular type of underground network with which we are all familiar. When construction began on the London Underground in the 1860s, however, it rang alarm bells with those who thought no good could come from delving into the bowels of the earth. The dire prediction of the Rev. Dr John Cumming was that 'the forthcoming end of the world will be hastened by the construction of the railways, burrowing into infernal regions and thereby disturbing the Devil.' His warnings were not heeded, and the Metropolitan Railway, the world's first underground rail network, was opened in 1863. Since then, the Tube network has been expanded to cover 250 miles of track across the Greater London area, tunnelling through plague pits, monasteries and Roman ruins. Up to five million people use the network on a daily basis, and few give any thought to what lurks beyond the safety of the Tube carriage as it rattles through miles of tunnel.

There are some, though, for whom the Underground network is a different world entirely. Every night, when the trains have stopped, the tracks are checked manually by Underground workers who walk them in the dark, armed only with cap lights. While you are clinging tightly to a pole, braced at an awkward angle so as to avoid an encounter with a tall man's armpit, a train driver is staring down the darkness of the tunnel alone. In a modern network like the Underground, we don't hear much tell of bluecaps, *coblynau* or fairies. However, those who work on the Tube certainly feel they are not alone. Perhaps the Rev. Cumming's concerns were not entirely without foundation.

Kennington Loop

Kennington Tube Station was, for many years, the final destination of most southbound trains on the snarled, tripartite Northern Line. The line's two northerly branches come together here before diverging again, like the proverbial two roads in a wood, and while some trains carry on south towards Morden, many used to turn around at Kennington and retrace their tracks in the opposite direction. In 2021, a long-awaited extension to the Northern Line opened. Now the majority of trains that would once have terminated at Kennington will continue instead through Nine Elms, carrying hip, sleek apartment-dwellers to their hip, sleek apartments (never *flats*) in the vast Art Deco building that was, in a former life, Battersea Power Station. Few southbound trains today make the lonely trek around the subterranean circle of track known as the Kennington Loop.

Train drivers like Alan greeted the news of the Battersea line extension with great cheer, not because they felt London needed more 'innovative mixed-use neighbourhood[s]' but because, to Alan's mind, every minute spent in the Kennington Loop is a minute too many.

For Tube enthusiasts – and there are many, many Tube enthusiasts – the Loop has something of a cult appeal. Perhaps it's the allure of the forbidden, of evading the TfL workers whose job it is to usher passengers off the train before it conducts its U-turn to arrive back at Kennington again, now pointing in the opposite direction. There's also a particular uniqueness about this, the only place in all of Tubeland where, should you miss your stop, there's a second chance to catch it before it moves on to the next station. Travelling the Loop deliberately, though, as part of a determined group, is an entirely different thing to travelling it as the sole passenger on the train. Despite the best efforts of train-evacuators at Kennington, it's certainly possible to do this unintentionally. My friend Tish, an avid podcast-devourer and regular Northern Line user, reports having been jolted back to reality on a number of occasions, only to discover she had accidentally travelled beyond the end of the line, into the liminal space of the Loop. She reported no hauntings – but then, she was never really alone on the train. None of us civilians will ever know the reality of being, entirely and completely, alone in the Loop.

Alan knows.

Alan has been driving Tube trains for twenty-seven years. He is the disembodied voice pleading with tourists to move down inside the carriage, or berating the backpacker whose £200 designer rucksack is preventing the door from closing. On the Northern Line, which remains non-automated, it is Alan who closes the carriage doors; and it is Alan who, when the train has been emptied at Kennington, pilots it into the darkness of the Loop, where it is held sometimes for fifteen minutes at a time.

In Kennington Loop, as the sole occupant of a train empty of all but its ghosts, fifteen minutes can seem very long indeed.

As a young train operator, Alan was quick to dismiss the stories others told: of the long-dead track-walkers with their gas lanterns, eternally walking their routes; of the screams still heard at Bethnal Green where, in 1943, 173 people were crushed to death during an air raid. Alan is a Londoner, as familiar with the Tube as with his own front street. The Underground, he thought, was not haunted. The notion was ridiculous.

By the time Alan had worked on the network for a year, he knew how wrong he'd been. What knowledge ordinary Londoners have of the Tube network is superficial, sanitised, contained to station platforms and within carriage walls. The underground world of train operators is another thing altogether, a labyrinth beneath London known to nobody but those whose job it is to keep it running. Like miners, Underground workers are a community of their own, leaving their homes daily to descend into the bowels of the earth; like miners, they are superstitious.

Anyone who has ever heard the internal doors on a Tube train being opened and shut will know that the sound it makes is like no other. It's a distinctive *ker-klunk, ker-klunk,* decidedly different from the *whoosh* of the external doors sliding into place. Nobody should be opening and closing internal doors on a Tube train without good reason. They certainly shouldn't be doing it on an empty train, held suspended in the darkness beyond Kennington, with nobody but Alan to hear the sound.

One evening in the late 1990s, Alan sat alone in the cab of a Northern Line train, awaiting the signal to move. The train had been emptied at Kennington. There were no sleepy drunks disoriented in the rear carriage; no late-night commuters too engrossed in their papers to have realised the train had terminated. There was no conductor. Definitively, unavoidably, Alan was alone on the train.

Ker-klunk. Ker-klunk.

In the silent embrace of the tunnel, the sound was as startling as a gunshot. Alan jerked upright in his seat. He was alone, he repeated mentally to himself; entirely alone. There was no possibility that anyone could have opened and closed a carriage door. Alan thought frantically, attempting to calm his racing heart. Noises carry strangely underground; could it be that the sound had come from another train, further up the track? It seemed unlikely, but then, any other suggestion seemed impossible.

Ker-klunk.

Closer. This sound was closer. Alan was by now familiar enough with his train to recognise that the initial *ker-klunk* had come from the rearmost set of doors and that this one, unmistakably, signified the next, moving towards the front of the train. The idea of unusual acoustics had to be abandoned. Somebody had opened and closed two internal doors. This was an unavoidable fact. And it hadn't been Alan.

Alan struggled to engage his brain. He clenched his fists tightly in his lap and tried to breathe. The train had been cleared at Kennington, but it was always possible that a mistake had been made, particularly if someone specifically did not want to be seen. This was a calming thought for five seconds before alarm bells rang again, thoughts of maniacs and assassins cannoning through Alan's head. What if—

Ker-klunk.

That was the next carriage. The period of time between the sounds seemed to have decreased. Alan glanced frantically between the cameras on his dashboard, looking for a stowaway, but there was nothing. Nobody. He was alone on the train.

Ker-klunk. Ker-klunk.

The sound was close behind him now, the doors to the front carriage opening and closing. Alan was paralysed. He closed his eyes. Perhaps this was it, his final moment. Any second now, whoever was travelling with him would burst into the operator's cab, and then—

The signal buzzed. Time to move. Alan exhaled, then inhaled near-desperately, his hands shaking wildly as he engaged the controls. Back to Kennington, and into the light. The brightness of the platform felt like benediction.

Alan was young, and had no desire to set himself up for mockery, but there was no question of keeping quiet when he stumbled, weak and white-faced, out of his cab. On the platform, a station-worker hastened to prop him up, then said – Alan will never forget it – 'Internal doors?'

Between them, they searched the train again. It was empty. Alan had, as he thought, been alone.

The station worker said he'd heard the story of the doors a thousand times from train operators, and they'd all worn the same expression upon emerging from the Loop that he'd seen on Alan's face. Someone had told him a passenger had been killed once, trying to board a train between the carriages. It might have been true.

*

There are few Underground staff, according to Alan, who don't have at least one unsettling story to tell. The 2005 documentary *Ghosts on the Underground,* directed by Joe Kane, bears this out: it features dozens of workers sharing their tales of lights in the tunnels, figures visible on CCTV cameras but not to the naked eye, and the eerie echoes of tragic long-ago stampedes. It also includes two accounts of the Kennington Loop horror, one of the most notorious Tubeland hauntings. When I spoke to Alan in Kennington Station, I asked him, half-casually, whether he'd heard the stories. This is what prompted him to recount his own experience above.

It isn't only workers, however, who have felt an uncanny tingle in Tubeland. By night, the long, tiled corridors and deserted platforms of many stations are unsettling in themselves, even before you consider the 49 disused 'ghost' stations which still lie along the 249 miles of the Underground network, untrodden for decades by passengers' feet.

You get onto the Tube; you get off the Tube; you make your way home. Usually. But people are killed on the Underground with horrifying regularity; perhaps there are many souls who enter the Tube network, but who never leave.

Ghost Train

In the early 2000s, Alison and her parents made the three-hour journey from Sheffield to see a concert in central London. Unfamiliar with the city – and generally horrified by the price tags of accommodation close to the venue – they booked a hotel in the Docklands area, on the far southern reaches of the Docklands Light Railway.

The concert was not the sort of big-ticket bonanza that draws tourists in their droves and leads afterwards to Tube station blockages that seem worryingly likely to end in fatalities. It was an up-and-coming indie band, finishing late on a Tuesday evening, and so when the family made their way to the nearest Tube station, it was nearly deserted.

They had a long journey ahead, necessitating a change midway, but with no bustling crowds to communicate urgency, they saw no reason to hurtle down the steep stairs or dash to the platform.

However, when they reached the platform just in time to see the rear end of a departing train, Alison's father Tom immediately regretted this decision, and expressed it bluntly in his body language.

His wife, Sarah, shook his arm soothingly and smiled. 'Don't worry – this isn't the sticks. There's another one due in nine minutes; look.'

The electronic board agreed with her. The next train was due in nine minutes. Tom relaxed somewhat, and availed himself of one of the plastic seats on the platform, rarely free during daylight hours.

Another couple drifted onto the platform, not speaking. The family group waited in companionable silence, pleasantly tired from the night's adventure.

Silence in a Tube station is broken gradually. First, there comes a very distant vibration, and then a humming from the lines deep within the tunnel as a train rattles over them, making them sing. Even for the relatively uninitiated, the rumble of an approaching train is unmistakable. Alison and her parents both looked up at the sound, what seemed to be an early and welcome surprise.

6 *minutes,* blared the board, but nevertheless, a train was quite evidently approaching. Alison could hear it thundering towards the platform and stepped back

automatically, lifting up her bag. This was a line with no diversions, so any train should have been suitable; but, out of instinct, she glanced at the front of the train as it surged out of the darkness.

There was nothing on the front. No destination; no indication. Alison hefted her rucksack onto her shoulder and furrowed her brow. Not familiar with London, she wondered whether she'd been mistaken in the past – was the destination not always listed? Did they only bother if there was more than one branch to the line?

She stepped back, watching the train chug up along the platform. The carriages, fluorescently lit, were empty. In some ways, this was unsurprising; the station itself was relatively empty. So, too, the streets above. But as the train continued to snake out of the tunnel, Alison was forced to correct herself. It wasn't *relatively* empty. It was completely, utterly deserted. No driver. The cab was empty.

A chill crawled slowly up the back of Alison's neck.

As the train drew closer, she reasoned that, perhaps, some trains were self-driving – she didn't know the ins and outs of how the Underground worked. The thought felt unconvincing, however; she turned to point it out to her father, but the cab was now out of sight.

Eventually, the train stopped. The doors opened. Tom, his bags already in hand, glanced back towards his wife and daughter encouragingly. 'Well?' he said. 'Come on!'

'We'll get the next one,' Sarah said quickly.

Tom halted in motion, face stilling. He opened his mouth as if to speak, but the expressions on the faces of his wife and daughter made him hesitate. When he glanced up the platform, he saw that the other couple, too, were hanging back, speaking to each other in low voices – making no move to approach the train.

'There was no driver,' Alison said weakly, glancing up at her mother. Wondering whether they'd seen the same thing.

Tom opened his mouth, then closed it again. 'Of course there's a bloody driver. It must've been a trick of the light.'

'We don't know where it's going,' Alison's mother protested, bludgeoning past Tom's disbelief. 'It didn't say on the front. We'll get the next one.'

Tom stood there a moment and then, subsiding, put his bag back down. 'Fine,' he said.

The train – naturally – seemed to stand for a long time on the platform, like a challenge. When it eventually began to surge once more into motion, Alison felt relief drop like a stone into the pit of her stomach. She looked up, slowly, at the empty train as it finally departed.

In the last carriage, an elderly woman stood anchored near the door, clinging to a vertical pole. As the train pulled out of the station, her eyes met Alison's and held them. A shadow swallowed her up; when it passed, the carriage was once again empty. The woman had disappeared.

180

The train chugged into the opposite tunnel and out of sight, back into the depths of the eternal underground.

*

Humans fear the dark. It's an atavistic, instinctive revulsion which, over millions of years of our existence, has caused us to inscribe figures in the dark places that exist below our living world. Perhaps we simply cannot conceive of a subterranean land with nobody in it. Perhaps it's more frightening, somehow, for such a place to be uninhabited.

What underworld inhabitants we imagine, however, are quite clearly shaped by our cultural perceptions. As a civilian Londoner, Alan was not privy to the deepest, darkest pockets of the Underground world, within which the imaginations of train operators have run wild for a century. As a casual miner, late to the game, Ritchie had no knowledge of knocker lore, but when the idea was put in his mind – well, then everything began to take shape.

It's the overground world which tells us which shape the underworld should form. The enduring *munacielli* of Napoli are a fascinating example because they represent a modern-day adherence to a fairy-type legend which is little-replicated in the United Kingdom. Until the mid-nineteenth century, we were a people in thrall to the Fair Folk, their residence under hill and down dale undeniable. Once inextricably intertwined with belief in witches, the concept of fairies has rather faded away – but we have still needed something to replace it. For as long as our underground wombs remain, we retain an instinctive need to plant something quasi-human in them.

We are not, of course, designed to be subterranean creatures. Perhaps this is part of why the underground world elicits such discomfort within us. In tunnels, caves and mines, whether natural or man-made, darkness reigns, obfuscating and enabling who knows what behaviours. The reputation of the underworld precedes it: it unnerves us, and so we populate it with beings who, depending on context, which may be post-human, sub-human, or non-human. We imagine our world in negative, the other side of the tape.

Alan's family was not one which believed. A pragmatic east Londoner, he was born within the echo of Bow Bells and trusts only in the evidence of his own senses. Below ground, however, these senses are heightened. On the Underground, a Londoner like Alan becomes part of a second, separate community, one which, like the miners to whom knockers were so important, has its own preoccupations. To Tube enthusiasts, Kennington Loop is a novelty; to Underground workers, it's a deeply haunted place. If Alan had not been greeted by a station worker who knew of the Loop's reputation, he might have put the experience out of his head entirely. Instead, though, the earlier hauntings were allowed to reinforce Alan's ordeal. Alan heard strange noises in the Kennington

Loop + the Kennington Loop is haunted = Alan was haunted by the ghost in the Kennington Loop.

What we find in our mines and Metros is also replicated in some private spaces which, however unwillingly or unwittingly, become public. If we enter the Kennington Loop, believing it to be haunted, we are hugely more likely to experience a haunting in the Kennington Loop. But what of private houses, stately homes, palaces whose entrenched spirits have become public knowledge? How do haunted houses haunt themselves?

A haunted house is only haunted for those who believe. I began researching this book after the reputedly haunted house in Elspeth Street, opposite my childhood dental practice, sold for the second time in as many years. If, like the indefatigable student in Naples, you resolutely ignore the spiritual rumours, living in a plagued house has more benefits than downsides. But if even the slightest element of trepidation enters the house with you, you must beware. *Caveat emptor.*

Like folklore, hauntings are self-perpetuating. A house known to be haunted can become a legal issue for its owners, as in the case of *Stambovsky v. Ackley (1991),* or can make the task of selling increasingly difficult. The question is, though – must there truly be a spirit in residence in such places? Is it not possible that haunted houses are plagued by nothing but their reputation? In Tibetan Buddhism, there originated a concept that has since spread to the realm of the paranormal – that of a tulpa, a being or thought-form created purely because so many people believe intensely in its existence. Can a house's reputation become a *tulpa* warping and reframe the place's image within the public consciousness? Does it matter whether a haunted house is haunted by anything other than its own influence?

Let's return to Elspeth Street.

Chapter Five
Private Property, Public Interest

SOME PEOPLE ARE TERRIFIED of the dentist. It's an anxiety I've never fully understood, but then, I didn't endure a childhood punctuated by tooth-pullings, brace-tightenings or flashes of the dentist's drill. Through the luck of the genetic draw, I have thirty-two solidly anchored teeth and a mouth big enough to contain them all – even my lower right wisdom tooth with its extra crenellations, a little Juliet balcony of bone. Were I to come to violence, my dentist would know me by my jawbone alone. Our teeth can still speak for us decades centuries – after our flesh is dust. If, unlike mine, your teeth have no natural oddities, it's often your dentist's handiwork you have to thank for this.

I have never felt a flicker of anxiety about my dentist. The tall Victorian townhouse in which the practice is housed still smells as comfortingly of cloves and cleaning fluid as it did in my earliest recollections; tiny iridescent fish still drift serenely about the brightly lit tank in the waiting room. The building is old, but it's cheerful, and untroubling.

The house opposite, though, is another story. This house is notorious. I've never been inside, but I, and many others, are fascinated by the experiences of those who have.

Last December, my annual Christmas check-up was the last appointment of the day before the holiday closure. It was raining hard, with a wind so stiff the water seemed to be travelling horizontally. The street outside the dentist's surgery was empty; behind a line of trees, the house across the way stood unlit, its darkened windows gazing grimly out at me as I hastened towards my car. At 4 p.m. on the cusp of Christmas, no stranger, I'm sure, would have glanced at the house twice; it's well kept, in a well-to-do area, and superficially unremarkable. But I am not a stranger. I may never have set foot in the house, but I have known it by reputation all my life.

That house, so they say, is haunted. Everybody's heard the stories, whose basis in truth only grows more convincing with every new family that moves into the property with brash enthusiasm and then departs at speed. There's something in there that shouldn't be – a voice in the walls, a shadow in the attic. Land Registry open data goes back only as far as 1995, but in those twenty-eight years, this house has been sold no fewer than six times. Property aggregation website themovemarket.com informs me with delightfully bland understatement that 'this house didn't turn out to be a great investment for its previous owner'. This sort of sales history would be enough to alarm a prospective buyer even without the rumour that the house comes with an un-evictable tenant; combine the two and you do indeed get an 'investment rating' of less than one star out of five.

The house opposite the dentist was one of the first reputed ghost nests ever to take root in my brain and burrow deep. As I've written about at length, the place I grew up in has no shortage of spooks and spectres, witches and White Ladies; tales of encounters with all of these were passed around at sleepovers and told as bedtime stories. Something about this house, though, struck me as different. For years, I peered up at its dark windows whenever I passed it, and wondered whether anyone was looking back. Everybody said the house was haunted – but if I were to ask the mother doing the washing-up in the kitchen, or the child kicking a football against the backyard wall, what would they say? Unlike the ruins of once-grand Gibside Hall, this house is, has been, and remains a private space. Some elements of what lie inside its walls have become public, to the extent that the reputation of the place precedes it whenever it comes to market. But it isn't a place into which I could take a camera crew and a ouija board. It's a place like other houses up and down the country, where homework has been rushed through at the dining room table, Christmas dinners have been laboriously cooked and riotous arguments have been had. *Reputation* places a sinister figure on the periphery of all these ordinary happenings when I, or other locals, think about the house, but is it really there? Does this reputation matter and, if so, to whom?

I first began working on this book in an attempt to pin down at least one first-hand story about what happens in the house that can't seem to hang on to its human inhabitants. I've managed that – but, I quickly realised, *what happens* in this or any haunted home is only the tip of an iceberg whose submerged bulk plunges far deeper than we might imagine.

The Boy in the Attic

When Beryl moved her family into the house on the hill, she didn't know it was haunted. In the mid-'90s, property listings were still communicated in pull-out sections of Sunday newspapers and via boards in estate agents' windows. Beryl – who was local, but not quite local *enough* – saw the house in a newspaper and marvelled at the price. Nothing in the north-east of England has ever been expensive, comparatively speaking, but this was something else. No narrow little end-terrace, this house was in grand Victorian style, high-ceilinged and possessed of character fireplaces and sweeping bannisters. It was the sort of house that had once expected to play host not only to a family, but a serving girl too. It was a middle-class house being advertised at a decidedly working-class price.

Beryl assumed there was something wrong with it, of course – damp, subsidence, black mould. But she was nothing if not aspirational, and mightn't it be worth a look? After all, whatever's wrong with a house can usually be fixed if the buyer is persistent enough.

This was an attitude that was to dictate Beryl's actions for several years to follow.

The survey turned up nothing that wouldn't be expected of a Victorian home. The walls were too old to have cavity insulation and the boiler was somewhat outdated. The windows were single-glazed, and having them replaced in similar style would be expensive. But these were mere niggles in the grand scheme of things. The house was structurally sturdy, aesthetically impressive, and even Beryl's dad could find no complaint to make other than that it would be hell to heat. Beryl decided that relative confidence from a pessimistic ex-builder was good enough to bet on, and put in an offer forthwith.

For a while, the house was something of a construction site. As winter set in and the windows rattled in their frames in the strong north-eastern wind, Beryl began to think she could see what the key issues were. The punishing gradient of the hill also made life difficult for builders' vans as they crawled towards the house heavily laden with new double-glazed windows, decorators' gear and damp-proof courses. The attic room, which had once been the servants' quarters, had been seized upon right away by Beryl's middle child, Andrew, but its anti-quated skylights leaked in the rain and the room was uninhabitable until good weather rolled around once more, allowing safe access to the roof. In the meantime, Andrew grumblingly shared with his younger brother on the first floor. There wasn't much between them but, at six, Andrew declared that four-year-old Sean was 'a baby', and yearned volubly for the day when his own room, with its novel slanted ceilings, would be ready for him. Beryl yearned, too. Things would be more settled then – or so she thought.

It was early April by the time Beryl, Andrew and Andrew's older sister Laura were able to ready the room for occupation. Hefting a bed up the narrow final flight of stairs was no mean feat. Beryl took comfort in the fact that the room, with its deep window seats and generous walk-in cupboard, required little additional furniture for storage. In a room like this, kitted out originally for maidservants who might be itinerant, everything you needed was already there. Built to last, Beryl thought, as she helped Andrew stow his toys in the top-opening window seat.

Beryl wasn't surprised to be woken in the night. Much as he'd clamoured for the move upstairs, Andrew had blinked awake, disoriented, several times since their arrival in the new house, apparently unsure of his surroundings. In the attic room, the trees cast strange shadows on the curtains and the bulk of Andrew's dressing gown, hanging on a clip on the outside of the cupboard door, was the sort of thing which might, in darkness, create the illusion of a human figure. When

Andrew called for his mother at midnight, Beryl fumbled for the nightlight Andrew had declared himself too old for and carried it up the stairs.

Andrew was huddled under the covers, clutching them over his head. At the sound of his mother's footsteps, he whimpered faintly, stopping only when she laid a warm hand on his shoulder and said his name.

'Hey,' she said, 'it's me. It's only me.'

When Andrew emerged from his cocoon, his face was red. He reached for the nightlight, placing it possessively on the brand-new bedside table.

'There was a boy in here,' Andrew said decisively. Beryl had been prepared for something along these lines.

'Is he still here now?'

Andrew glanced nervously over her shoulder, then ducked his head again. 'No.'

Andrew pointed in the direction of the walk-in cupboard. Beryl tried not to smile. Of course she shouldn't have hung the dressing gown there until Andrew was used to the shape of the room, the way the darkness and the light moved through it. The cupboard door was slightly ajar, so Beryl got up with the intention of shutting it.

'Don't,' Andrew protested, and Beryl realised that he was more afraid of her *opening* it.

'Was he in here?' she asked, and Andrew nodded tightly.

'Hmm.' Beryl opened the door confidently, revealing Andrew's child-sized clothes hanging on child-sized hangers, various boxes stacked neatly underneath. 'Not much room in here, is there?'

Andrew shook his head. The covers were still clutched beneath his chin.

Beryl closed the door, then gestured to the dressing gown on the back of it. 'Do you think it might have been this you saw? Our eyes get confused in the dark, you know.' She unhooked the garment and draped it over the back of the chair before, thinking better of it, she returned to the cupboard, hung it up on a hanger and closed the door.

Andrew watched the proceedings warily. Beryl smiled at him, then crossed the room again to perch on the edge of his bed.

'It was just a shadow,' she said, stroking the blond hair back from the small face. 'See? Go back to sleep.'

Andrew didn't wake again. When Beryl went up in the morning to open the curtains, though, she noticed that the cupboard door was once again standing open. She frowned and pushed it closed. She couldn't imagine Andrew having got out of bed in the night after his upset, and that meant an uneven floor or, perhaps, a loose latch. She sighed. Something else to fix.

It took Andrew a few weeks to become used to the room. Over that period, he would call for Beryl every other night, at first, and then every other two. Each time, Beryl would come upstairs, turn on the nightlight, and open the cupboard door fully so Andrew could see inside. The dressing gown had long since been hung elsewhere, so now, Beryl supposed, it was the creak of the cupboard door opening – and then the slit of unfathomable darkness inside – which set Andrew off. It was the boy, Andrew said, who opened the door. Beryl thought it was probably her own steps in the bathroom on the floor below as she prepared for bed, unsettling the old house and making the latch fail.

'There's no little boy here,' Beryl would say patiently. 'Just you.'

'There is,' Andrew insisted stubbornly, so Beryl tried a different tack.

'Does he hurt you?'

'No,' Andrew admitted. 'He just stands there.'

Beryl tried to ignore the way this thought made her skin crawl. She'd been unsettled by enough heaps of laundry in her time to know the dark could play ridiculous tricks.

'Well,' she said, 'I don't think there's really a boy. But if there is, you just ignore him. He obviously doesn't mean any harm. All right?'

'All right,' Andrew capitulated.

As the weeks went on and summer came, the night-time upsets decreased in frequency until they stopped altogether. Beryl put this down to the lighter evenings and earlier mornings, as well as to the fact that Andrew now knew his room very well indeed. The cupboard door had his artwork Blu Tacked to it. A frieze of dinosaurs ran around the centre of the room, dividing the walls into blue (above) and green (below). This was Andrew's room now. He was no longer afraid of it.

One weekend, Beryl decided that the more pressing things in the house had all been done and it was time to sort the niggle of the loose latch on Andrew's cupboard door. It had become such a habit for her to push the door closed in the mornings that she now did it almost without thinking, but it would be nice to feel that everything was *perfect,* rather than simply good enough. A handyman was called, the old latch unscrewed and a new one affixed in its place. Beryl jiggled it and felt confident that not only would it not come unlatched on its own, it was far too stiff for Andrew's little fingers to manage. That meant the top shelf of the cupboard could offer valuable hiding space for Christmas presents once Beryl started buying this year's stash in earnest.

When night came, Andrew blithely watched her demonstrate the latch and agreed that it was much nicer than the rusted thing it had replaced. After a moment, though, a look of concern flickered over his face.

'What if he can't open it?'

'Who?' Beryl asked, confused.

'The boy,' Andrew explained patiently. 'He doesn't like the door closed at night.'

Beryl frowned. 'I thought you weren't scared to sleep here now? You've been so good.'

'I'm not *scared,*' Andrew said. 'He just wants the door open.'

Beryl pushed down a surge of alarm. 'Well,' she said, 'I want it shut. All right?'

Andrew looked uncertain, but got into bed. 'All right.'

In the morning, Beryl had reached out for the door and pushed it habitually closed before she realised: first, that it shouldn't be open; and second, that the new latch required her to turn a knob before she could press it home again. Her fingers stilled for a moment on the stainless steel before she recovered enough to manipulate the mechanism.

Andrew was stirring in bed, pulling himself upright. Beryl looked over at him in dull confusion.

'Did you open this door?' she demanded.

'No,' Andrew said, 'I can't reach.' He thought for a moment. 'It must've been the boy.'

He looked brightened by this prospect. Beryl was not. She called the handyman back and explained the situation.

The handyman looked unimpressed. 'Are you trying to get a refund out of me or what?' He rapped on the door, then walked around in a circle on the floorboards, his steps heavy and measured. 'This thing isn't going anywhere.'

Beryl considered. 'I thought it might be movement downstairs that did it.'

'Go and move downstairs, then,' said the handyman.

Beryl did. She tugged at the bannister, stomped on the landing, leaned heavily against the wall immediately below the cupboard. The latch held firm, and so did the handyman.

'Must be your lad,' he said, putting his tools back into their case. 'They're always cleverer than we think, you know.'

Beryl didn't doubt this, but there was cleverness and then there was basic dexterity and strength. Andrew could not have unlatched the door, and for his sister, Laura, to have crept up two flights of creaking stairs to do it would have been virtually impossible without waking Beryl, quite apart from the fact that it made no sense.

The boy didn't like to have the cupboard closed. This thought sat uneasily in Beryl's gut. In the handyman's absence, she felt suddenly and strangely observed in the empty attic. She unlatched the door again, just in case, and left it that way. Perhaps it was better not to know.

For months, she existed in a state of not-knowing, made easier by the hecticness of life with three children under ten. By the time autumn arrived and the prospect of Christmas loomed distressingly close, she could almost tell herself she'd imagined it all: the mysterious boy and the door that unclosed itself. It was silly, and that cupboard would make the best childproof hideaway in the house.

One night in early December, when she put Andrew to bed, she latched the door. By the following morning, something or someone had unlatched it again.

Beryl decided not to think about it. Not thinking about it had worked for a while, anyway; now she simply had to put her mind to it with greater dedication. Every night, the cupboard was latched; it never seemed to unlatch itself during the day, a thought upon which Beryl refused to dwell. Every morning, or almost, she would snick the door shut again. Out of sight, out of mind.

One evening when the nights had begun to draw in, Beryl left the children with her sister so she could do some Christmas shopping without having to perform a laborious pantomime of secrecy. Upon her return, she parked her car, as she always did, on the hill above her house. The evening was dim, but not yet dark, and as Beryl approached the house, she paused to admire it silhouetted against the fading light: the slender arms of the leafless trees; the newly neat garden. On the side of the house that faced her, right at the top of the house, was the attic window. As she raised her eyes to it, she could just make out an unfamiliar shape.

She blinked, and the shape resolved itself into the figure of a boy.

Beryl froze. Only this sensation of being literally frozen in place prevented her from dropping her bags in the street. Instead, she stood in the middle of the road, staring up at the window and willing the shape to reveal itself as something else. But it didn't. There was a boy in the attic, just as Andrew had said.

After what seemed a very long time, the door to the dentist's office opposite opened and a family spilled noisily into the thickening evening. The sound of their chatter seemed to free Beryl from some strange thrall. One moment the boy was there, and the next, the window was empty.

Beryl had intended to put the Christmas presents in the attic room cupboard, but now this possibility seemed as remote as the moon. Unlocking her front door with shaking hands, she stuffed her bags hastily behind a mess of clutter stowed under the stairs. She could move them later.

It seemed a very long time before the children arrived home. That evening, as Beryl put Andrew to bed, she tugged back the curtains and examined the room from various angles, seeking out anything – a mislaid toy; a pile of washing – which might have appeared as a shape in the window, but there was nothing. Andrew grew impatient, demanding story time, so Beryl gave up the attempt as a bad job and slipped under the covers with him, opening *The Wind in the Willows*.

On her way out, she unlatched the cupboard door.

They never spoke about the boy again. Beryl never saw a reprise of the vision in the window, but then, she took care never to look up at it when passing in the dark and, moreover, she never resumed latching the cupboard door. She found another place for the Christmas presents.

Beryl's visitors always admired the house, and Beryl agreed that it was beautiful. Doors didn't slam at night. Children didn't cry. But sometimes, Beryl would wake in a cold sweat and think about her middle child grown so used to the boy in his room that he took no notice. She would think about him standing in the cupboard, perfectly still, wanting nothing but for the door to be open for him.

The house was good enough, but it had a niggle now that couldn't be eradicated. Beryl persisted until she felt she couldn't. The limit of her endurance was four years.

When the house went on the market, the estate agent asked, as is rote, why they were selling. Beryl said that it was just a bit too big for them, and hard to keep on top of. Perhaps it would suit a family with more children.

The Boy (Still) in the Attic

Andrea and her husband bought the house from Beryl in mid-1999.

Beryl had mentioned the 'ghost' to friends, but always with the caveat that she was 'probably being silly'. The house had none of the structural or cosmetic issues that had been there when Beryl bought it. Andrea agreed that Beryl was undoubtedly telling tall tales, and knew her only tangentially. The house seemed a steal.

There wasn't much of a story to tell, Andrea said. 'We didn't believe in the ghost story, so we bought it. Our son said there was a boy in the attic who stared at him. He wouldn't be talked out of it. He cried every night, and then none of my other kids would swap with him, so we sold it. They hated that house.'

Was there a boy in the attic?

Andrea wouldn't quite be drawn. 'The kids said so.'

And you weren't willing to make the attic the master bedroom?

Andrea laughed. 'No. I'd have been imagining him all the time, looking at me. I don't really believe in ghosts, but . . .'

The pair sold the house in early 2000. They owned it for a grand total of five months.

*

The house opposite the dentist's is, in many ways, a classic case of a private place whose local reputation, once established, has snowballed over time with demonstrable real-world effects, whatever the veracity of the claims. Each rumoured ghost story grates like grit in an oyster and, over the years, various half-manufactured tales have been born like natural pearls, each with its own variations. Every time the house is sold, the stories are reinforced, and every time the stories are reinforced – and shared in pubs and playgrounds – the house seems to run a greater risk of being sold again. There may or may not be a boy in the attic, but many people *believe* there is – and therein lies the problem.

You may have encountered the term 'hyperstition'. Technically speaking, this is a neologism mostly applied to the sphere of techno-capitalism, but really it expresses an idea similar to the concept of chaos magic: the capacity of humans to will something into existence through belief alone, distorting reality through the power of group belief in an alternative truth. Coined by researchers at the Cybernetic Culture Research Unit, the term 'hyperstition' is typically applied to convictions which engender feedback cycles so powerful that they literally reshape our cultural fabric. As Nick Land puts it in *Catacomic* (1995), 'The hyperstitional object is no mere figment or "social construction" but it is in a very real way "conjured" into being by the approach taken to it'.

The phenomenon that Land is describing relates to some key aspects of modern society, in which we are all expected to believe. Consider the stock market: once upon a time, the value of money was routinely tethered to a gold standard, something which could be tangibly held in one's palm. Today, however, the economies of the world are fuelled almost entirely by anticipation and belief – we *think* of the value of money, and therefore, money has that value (or, as it more often seems these days, money hasn't). In recent years, this was illustrated clearly by the impact of the 'kamikaze' UK budget in autumn 2022, in which then-Chancellor Kwasi Kwarteng announced a series of unfunded tax cuts for corporations and high earners. This unexpected announcement so unsettled global markets that it instantly plunged the country into a state of financial turbulence, with the pound at record lows and mortgage rates at mountainous highs. Many of the measures announced in the budget were swiftly reversed – it wasn't even enacted. *Nothing actually happened,* and yet the effect of economists' fears was nevertheless made manifest in real terms, felt not just on the stock market but at the level of individual households. Things could not simply return to the way they had been before the budget was announced because, although nothing had changed in our *physical* reality, it is not in the world of physical reality that twenty-first century economies live. What economists believe or anticipate, whether or not these things are true, can have catastrophic and long-lasting real-world effects, particularly in the financial arena.

We can see the same thing happening on a smaller scale in the case of the house opposite the dentist's office.

201

This house is liable to be a poor investment – whether or not there is really a restless spirit within its walls. What matters is that people *believe* there is. This sort of thing has been a pattern the world over, particularly in areas where superstition runs high; so-called 'stigmatised' homes can be so difficult to sell that dedicated agencies, such as California's Past Life Homes, have been founded especially to help struggling owners shift their cursed piles. While there is no state in the USA which specifically insists that the presence of a spirit in a property must be disclosed, in the case of 'open or notorious hauntings', Past Life founder Cindi Hagley says that these must go on the record to avoid falling foul of more general laws surrounding 'stigmatised property'. 'If it affects the material value of the home, it must be disclosed,' Hagley says.

Sometimes, of course, it isn't a sale that supposed ghost hosts are after. While a lively sales history can stoke the fires of superstition in a neighbourhood willing to entertain the possibility of spectral subletters, the complete absence of a sales history can have a similar effect. The human impulse – as seen in the mines, catacombs and railway tunnels of the world – seems to be to sketch sentience into dark places. The same is often true of *secret* places; private places; places whose stones we are forced to leave unturned. When a house frequently changes hands, we wonder what the sellers are running from. When a house has *never* been sold, though, but stands most of its life empty? Then we might begin to wonder what skeleton, what spectre, what sinister family secret the owners are keeping *in*.

*

In the county of Anglesey, off the rocky coast of North Wales, stands Craig Y Môr. This is its *name,* which does not much equate with *what it is called.* To those who live in the local area, the place has long been known as the Spooky House.

It isn't difficult to see why. Built between 1911 and 1919, it became a Grade II-listed building in 1998 as a 'prominent coastal landmark ... ambitious in scale, dramatic in massing, and refined in detail'. It's possible that bombastic television presenter Timmy Mallett – a colourful weekend memory for those of us of a certain age – more fully captured the thoughts of the masses when he visited the headland on a painting expedition in 2022. 'Is this the *Psycho* house?' he tweeted. 'Spooky.'

Anyone familiar with Hitchcock's 1960 film will spot the similarities in aspect between the Spooky House and the austere Bates Motel. Dramatically positioned at height, Craig Y Môr occupies what looks a somewhat perilous location on the coast of Holy Island in Trearddur Bay. Holy Island is a smaller, more isolated adjunct to the Isle of Anglesey itself; not only does Craig Y Môr sit on the peripheries of a nation, it is anchored so close to the edge of the headland that it appears one rock fall away from being claimed by the sea. This is not actually true: the structural integrity of the house, and the cliff itself, have never been questioned. The psychological effect, however, is powerful. Craig Y Môr sits on the edge of the world.

Anglesey – or, to give it its correct Welsh name, Ynys Môn – is a place that has been well known for its superstition since the eleventh century (when, one imagines, the bar was set rather higher in terms of how much superstition was too much). Hugh Lupus, the Norman Earl of Chester, reputedly made an attempt to silence the 'superstitious Welsh' when he heard tell of Maen Morwydd, or 'the Thigh Stone', which supposedly would always return to its mother altar in Llanidan Church, even if submerged in the Menai Strait. Lupus had his men throw the stone into the sea. The following morning, they found it sitting on the altar, briny-wet and strewn with seaweed. The stone is now embedded in the walls of the church. Superstition in Ynys Môn cannot be so easily killed.

With a house like the Spooky House casting its long shadow on the coast of Holy Island, this is still more true. Unlike the Bates Motel, this house has been a private residence from its earliest beginnings, never leaving the hands of the family for whom it was designed and built. It has had only three owners: after the death of its first, William Smellie, in 1955, it passed into the hands of his daughter Ruth, and thence to her children. Today, the house is occasionally used as a filming location; it featured in the 2015 ITV drama *Safe House*. It has never been open to the public – this is not a house one can lawfully enter without good reason. During the Second World War, it briefly played host to soldiers stationed on the island. But the sense of mystery around the Spooky House has been banked by all the years through which those on the island have been forced to look at its ominous exterior without being privy to what lies inside.

In many ways, it's a Gothic cliché. William Smellie, an Englishman – an outsider – had the house built initially as a summer house. Eventually, the family took more regular possession, but for long periods each year, the house seemed to remain empty, prompting rampant gossip as to what might be wrong with it. A haunting was the community's general conclusion, and this conclusion was only reinforced by the owners' edict that no local was supposed to set foot in the property.

Teenagers, of course, will always find a way.

Truth or Dare

The early 1970s on Holy Island were not exactly replete with hip and happening activities for the young. Without nightclubs, fashionable hang-out joints, or easy access to bigger, less isolated communities, the youth of the island resorted to the same forms of entertainment as rural teenagers everywhere – namely, drinking illicit alcohol in the dark and engaging in daft games and wild speculation. When it came to the Spooky House, that speculation was very wild indeed.

Everybody, according to Rhys, knew somebody who *knew somebody* who'd been into the house. Nobody seemed to have met a successful housebreaker first hand. One night in 1973, Rhys and his friends laid out the various stories they'd heard like cards on the metaphorical table, only to find that the points of overlap were few.

One salient point of connection, however, did exist.

Steve's friend of a friend had crept into the Spooky House via the basement, which could be broken into, he said, with little effort. Paul had heard the same. Through the basement window, it was possible to slip unnoticed into the always quiet, presumed empty house, and discover what was inside. It was trespassing, of course, but if the boys all wanted anything, it was to find out what else might be trespassing in Craig Y Môr. Where there was smoke, they thought, there must be some kind of fire.

The thing about Craig Y Môr was that the smoke was deeply inconsistent in nature. The house was thought of as ominous, oppressive, bizarre and, yes, *haunted*. However, the specifics of what haunted it were rarely discussed. In the grand scheme of things, after all, it was a relatively new house, completed after the First World War. Somebody had once overheard that the house had a soldier still living in it, long after Hitler's defeat in the Second. Stories varied as to whether he was a flesh and blood deserter who had run away and taken up residence in the house, where he now lived feral and AWOL in the basement, or whether he was long gone and yet not gone, the last lingering shreds of a person. Rhys thought this story was too woolly to be accurate. It wasn't that he didn't believe in ghosts; it was just that, usually, a haunted house has a certain cast of characters that recur – a shadow on the stairs or a woman at the window. The Spooky House seemed to be haunted by the fact that it was haunted. Nobody knew what went on inside it. That, in the end, was the point.

It was wet and warm on the night Rhys's friends decided someone should storm the fortress. Even in midsummer, the night air on Holy Island is cool and clean with sea fret, but the heat of the day still lingered enough that it was bearable to sit in a T-shirt and gaze at the silhouette of the Spooky House, way up on the cliff.

'I don't believe anyone's really been in there,' Rhys said – famous last words.

'D'you want to bet on it?' Steve said. 'I bet you can get in through the basement. I dare you.'

A sensible person would have laughed off this suggestion for their own self-preservation, but Rhys was, at the time of the incident, a fifteen-year-old boy. Of course there was never any possibility of sense entering the equation.

The small group crept across the island together. The idea, such as it was, was for the group to poke around the base of the house until they found a likely route in. Then, Steve and Paul would keep watch while Rhys, as per the terms of the dare, ventured inside. If it was interesting (and safe), he would return to beckon the others in. If it was *un*safe – well, they would cross that bridge when they came to it.

'Don't get murdered by the soldier,' Steve said brightly, as they neared the house.

To Rhys's mild distress, the route in was surprisingly easy to locate. Having spent some minutes arguing fervently that stories of Craig Y Môr's conquerors had been greatly exaggerated, he now had to accept that it was, actually, simple enough to get into the basement. He supposed the family mustn't live here all the time – but wasn't there anything of value in the house? Shouldn't it be more secure?

'I bet,' Steve said – he was a betting man these days – 'that once you're in, you won't be able to get up into the actual house, but worth a look, isn't it?'

Like Scooby Doo, Rhys thought dourly. He only hoped that, should he come across anything worrying, he'd be able to pull off its mask like Fred and then escape via the nearest window.

'Worth a look,' he echoed, with a growing lack of enthusiasm. 'If a ghost gets me, my Mam'll have your head.'

Landing light-footed in the basement felt like an anticlimax. After all these years of gazing at, muttering about, and dreading the house, now here Rhys was inside it, the moon streaming whitely through the high windows onto the dark floor. The basement itself was, as he'd imagined, filled with clutter, but he couldn't picture a mad soldier living in it. It smelled of must and iron. The air tasted like an old coin on the tongue.

The first few steps Rhys took were taken in comparative confidence. It wasn't until he was halfway across the room – closer to the staircase that led up into the house than he was to the window that led to safety – that he began to feel the pressure in his chest.

At first, he thought it was his imagination. Trespassing alone in the basement of the most mysterious house on the island, it was no surprise that his pulse was picking up, his throat feeling nervous and close. However, with every step he took, the feeling intensified. Rhys recollected it as something akin to a weight on his shoulders, on his lungs – or a band tightening around his chest. On this warm summer night, too, he could feel the temperature dropping precipitously around him. By the time he reached the stairs, his feet felt like lead, the muscles were clenching weakly in his thighs, and the hairs on his arms were standing on end.

Rhys didn't want to admit that there was anything in the basement, but, as he stood with his back to the cavernous room, the back of his neck felt exposed, vulnerable in a peculiarly awful way. It was as if someone was looking at him. Rhys knew, as we all know, when someone was looking.

Trepidation froze him to the spot. For some moments, Rhys stood unmoving, listening to the whipping of the wind around the house above. The sea roared in and out; as he listened, Rhys began to pick out something else, within and under the sound. Inside the basement, something that echoed the wind and the tide – in, and out. In, and out.

Rhys's own breathing quickened. Behind him, the other sound retained its unsettling regularity.

In, out. In, and out.

It was as if, Rhys said, the house itself was breathing.

Paul's voice shattered the rhythm. 'Rhys? Are you dead in there?'

Rhys isn't sure what it would've taken to bring him back to reality had Paul not stuck his brazen head through the window to call for him. His muscles were tightly clenched, his jaw stiff with tension. Around him, the cool air seemed to move like a living thing, but Paul's voice was a tether to the world outside and gave him the strength to speak.

'Here!' he said, ragged and thick.

From above, he heard the rejuvenating burst of Paul and Steve's laughter.

'Is there anything down there?' asked Paul.

'Yes,' said Rhys, with sudden unshakable surety. 'Yes!'

They guided him back to the window with low calls and encouragement, as one might coax a frightened dog. As he picked his way with eyes closed in the direction of the sound, Rhys spared a thought to be grateful that his friends, while cruel enough to send him into the house, were also compassionate enough to know when too far was too far. If Rhys said the house was haunted, they would believe him. For the most part, they already believed, anyway.

The sea air after dark would usually feel bracing at first upon emergence from any kind of structure, but this night, as Rhys heaved himself up onto the grass, it felt blissfully warm, soothing the goosepimples on his arms and neck. As he lay on his back on the ground and breathed deeply, the other two closed the window, looking down at him with barely restrained curiosity.

Rhys could feel his breathing returning to normal, his chest expanding. The band of tension was dissipating. Above him, the sky was full of stars.

'So,' Steve said, when he could bear it no longer, 'is it haunted?'

'Yes,' Rhys said firmly. 'Go in and see for yourself if you don't believe me.'

Both Steve and Paul, interestingly enough, declined this offer.

*

Fifty years later, Rhys is a middle-aged man far removed from that reckless boy on the island, and he regrets having so recklessly entered the Spooky House. But he insists he was far from alone in this misstep. Over the years, others have confessed their own trespasses in the oppressive basement. One man even claimed to have made it beyond the basement and into the house itself, which he found to be full of grandfather clocks.

This may or may not be true. The house today has a sparse website featuring views of various dark-panelled rooms and, oddly, numerous angles on a bathroom towel-rail. Pipework and stairs feature heavily, with one vertiginous shot depicting a stone spiral of steps from directly above. There are no grandfather clocks to be seen, but other deeply Gothic elements appear across the limited range of photographs: a portrait of the sort whose eyes would surely follow you across the room; a mechanism once used to summon servants to specific areas of the house but which, today, might be operated by an unseen hand. One image, in unsettling black and white, shows a wooden chair, askew, in a narrow, brick-walled room, like the aftermath of an interrogation. It's the sort of place that could rake in fistfuls of cash for owners willing to open it up to paranormal investigators and ghost hunters, but the website tersely stipulates that it is 'available for hire as a photo shoot and film location only'. A contact form invites the user to request further information, but the inquiry I submitted as to the local rumours of hauntings went unanswered.

Perhaps the owners of Craig Y Môr simply have nothing to say on the subject. It's entirely possible that, to them, it's nothing more than a family pile built in eclectic style by a much-loved grandfather, so familiar that its creaking stairs and ticking clocks barely register. Perhaps the house's local reputation is baffling to them – after all, they have never been in the position of an outsider looking in, imagining the sprawling building as a Welsh House of Usher, its walls teeming with sinister secrets. The images they choose to show seem to be curated to show the house in the eeriest possible light – but perhaps that's simply how we expect to see it? In one image, I see a rusting pipe clinging precariously to a stone wall, which might, in a horror film, be made to rattle atmospherically. An architect or buildings enthusiast might simply note the intricate and well-preserved early twentieth-century pipe-work. It is, like all things, a matter of perspective.

There is no doubt that Trearddur Bay is haunted by the Spooky House. Generations of young people in Porth yr Afon, which it overlooks, recall the looming shadow it cast over their childhood imaginations and, in some cases, investigations. Yet there are no consistent reports of specific spectres or apparitions around the home. Mostly, what is reported is a feeling of dread, a heaviness, a drop in temperature. Rhys felt something in the basement with him – but could it have been the force of hyperstition alone?

Such is the hold of a house like Craig Y Môr over a community like Porth yr Afon that it generates and regenerates a dark force of its own; it's little wonder that a teenage boy, alone in its grasp, might feel physic-ally unsettled, *visited* by his own terror of it. The house's suggestively Gothic aspect, alongside its private nature, combine to transform it into something beyond the sum of its parts. A house like this is both haunted and haunting, whether or not there is anything paranormal living in it.

Gothic imagery and tropes are so much a part of our cultural consciousness that it's natural for our brains to make associations between elements of a building – high staircases; dark wood panelling; antique portraiture; trap-doors; peripheral spaces like attics and cellars – and what we have seen or read in stories and films which use these recognised elements to unsettle us. The Spooky House has become locally defined by its neo-Georgian style, now widely viewed as 'creepy'. But there are other once private places which cast long shadows over communities not because of their austere architectural features, but because of atrocities suspected – or known – to have taken place there. Craig Y Môr has developed a life of its own simply because it looks as if it might have been the setting for a horror story.

In contrast, Newsham Park Hospital, in Tuebrook, Liverpool, is notorious in part because we *know* that it was.

*

Newsham Park began life as an orphanage for the children of seamen. Built at around the same time as nearby children's home Strawberry Field (1870), the buildings' afterlives – and resonance – could not have been more different. Popularised in the Beatles' song, Strawberry Field, owned by the Salvation Army, is now a visitor attraction boasting a training centre for young people with special educational needs. Newsham Park, meanwhile, became a psychiatric hospital in 1954, and then a self-described 'lunatic asylum' in the mind-bogglingly late year of 1992, before being sold to a property developer five years later. Various plans have been circulated; the group who took on the building in 2007 intend to turn it, so they say, into an 'events venue'. In reality, however, Newsham Park has been abandoned for twenty-six years, during which time it has become notorious as one of Britain's most haunted sites.

Liverpool, like its cultural neighbours Newcastle to the north and Cardiff to the south, is a city steeped in sentiment and inherited Celtic sensibilities – the sort of place where hauntings are approached by many as pragmatically as any other infestation. The *Liverpool Echo,* with characteristic understatement, observes that 'there are lots of spooky happenings in Merseyside'. From the poltergeist of Penny Lane to the nocturnal whisperings recorded at Croxteth Hall, ghosts and ghost belief abound here, in a casual way familiar to me from my own childhood. Little wonder, then, that such a community should have fixated on a site like Newsham Park, a towering relic of an age of so-called 'medicine' whose practices are now almost universally recognised as abhorrent. How, if we believe in ghosts, could there fail to be a bevy of them here?

Madness, or mental illness, has always been culturally connected to the Gothic – think of the first Mrs Rochester, the 'mad woman in the attic' who doubles as a metaphor for all Rochester's buried sins in *Jane Eyre*; or the protagonist of Charlotte Perkins Gilman's 'The Yellow Wallpaper', whose hysteria combines with the pressures of patriarchy to lock her in an inescapable mental prison. However, it is only in a world where the asylum has become a thing of the *past* that the functional trappings of mental hospitals themselves – creaking gurneys; bathchairs; tables used for electroshock therapy – have been viewed as more horrific than therapeutic, becoming staple props of the horror genre.

For many years, Newsham Park was, in its own way, a private home, which is why its cultural aftermath is relevant here. Orphans lived there, in a time when an orphanage was not a bizarre concept. Psychiatric patients lived there, in a time of regular institutionalisation. Only when the building was abandoned did it become possible for the public to see inside, by which point it represented not only itself, but an entire era of social attitudes now rightly deemed unacceptable. Newsham Park is an objectively eerie place, but the weight of its history makes it infinitely more haunting in 2024 than it would have been in 1924, when the memories it held had not yet become skeletons in society's closet.

Rumours of hauntings at Newsham Park date back to the time of its regular use. One former worker told the *Echo* in 2022 that there were whole wings of the building where staff were terrified to go, and that he himself had once seen the apparition of a white-coated man in the basement, especially notable due to his lack of a head. Since the place's abandonment, however, its relationship to the surrounding community has altered. Notices dating to 1996 can still be seen on the walls; trolleys stand askew in the corridors, where they were left at the end of long-gone staff's last shifts in the asylum. A locked room now laid open to the elements, Newsham Hall is a vast time capsule. If the tools of its early-'90s trade still linger there, it's natural to wonder whether some of its occupants might still linger within its halls too, shackled there by the weight of their pain.

Newsham Park's notoriety as a haunted house is such that ghost tours are now regularly run there – if you can squeeze your way onto the waiting list. According to locals like Liam, though, no thrill-hunter on an organised tour could ever appreciate how terrifying it was to enter Newsham Park unauthorised and alone, in the years before ghost business was booming.

'We didn't know what to expect,' Liam explains, 'but we expected *something*. And we got it.'

The Children

The boys had come in through the front door. Armed with bolt cutters and a hammer pilfered from somebody's shed, they'd expected Newsham Park to put up more of a fight, but the sidings around it were easily scaled and the door, when they reached it, had been forced open by some previous visitor. Nobody had attempted to seal it up again. Perhaps the disturbance had not even been noticed. Though the place was owned, it belonged not so much to *someone* as to a corporate entity so faceless it was more some*thing* – and this something didn't seem in much of a hurry to dedicate itself to Newsham Park's protection.

The entrance hall was far from welcoming. Part of this was doubtless related to the pervasive smell of mould and the chill drifting in through several shattered windows, but Liam couldn't imagine anyone ever entering Newsham

Park and feeling relieved to be home. The electric supply had been disconnected, but the moon was sufficiently full that the boys barely needed their torches to pick their way through the debris that littered the place. The lower-level windows were secured with metal grilles, and the air felt heavy, as if the barometric pressure had shifted at the threshold.

What startled Liam was the incongruity between the hulking, Gothic exterior of the hall and its blandly institutional innards. The white paint was cracked and peeling, but the dark swing doors, with their protective metal kickboards and signs declaring FIRE ALARM and GENERAL OFFICE, were a disturbing reminder that the place had been, until very recently, in regular use. Hatch windows allowed the boys to peer into desolate wards. In one cavernous room stood several rows of plastic chairs, as if they had been set up to receive a group of patients who would never arrive.

As the boys pressed deeper into the bowels of the building, Liam began to feel overheated and tense, as if he had a fever. The sight of a metal bedstead on its side in one small room made his heart rate spike even before he spotted the mirror on the wall – on it, in lipstick, some comic genius had inscribed the words 'LOOK BEHIND YOU'.

Instinctively, Liam recoiled, which sparked a chain reaction as he stumbled into the person behind him.

'Come on,' he said, 'let's get out of here' – and although the group were aware that the scrawl on the mirror was of human provenance, nobody objected. In a place like this, it was easy to be unsettled – in fact, *being unsettled* was the default state.

They had planned to venture downstairs into the morgue. An older friend claimed to have gone there once and allowed himself to be filed into one of the stainless steel body drawers. Earlier, in the daylight, Liam had been enthused by this plan, but now he felt he'd like to get as far away from the basement as possible. He brushed his fingers against his friend's arm and said, 'Shall we go upstairs?'

As the group ascended, Liam began to feel lighter, and at first, he was sure he'd made the right suggestion. Then, at a certain point, he realised that the lightness was light-headedness. It was at this moment that he heard, close to his ear, the unmistakable sound of a child's laugh.

Liam stumbled at once into the wall, clinging to the bannister. Below him, he could hear the others muttering; someone at the rear shouted out, 'Keep moving!'

Liam was a few steps above the others. Could it be that nobody else had heard? Liam put a hand to his chest, but to try and turn now would be social suicide, quite apart from the logistical difficulty. He was keyed up, he told himself. He was anticipating voices, and the distinct stirring of the air around his cheek and neck was a figment of his imagination.

He pressed on.

As the boys mounted the stairs, however, the sense of unease began to spread down through the group. Liam

219

could feel it. It didn't help that the staircase had transitioned from institutional lino-covered steps to a spiral steel affair which creaked and clanged beneath their feet. The noise of their ascent was enough to obscure any other sounds. Liam couldn't tell if this thought cheered or terrified him. More than once, he felt the hairs on the side of his face stand up. Soon enough, he was climbing with eyes closed, an old trick he'd used as a child to get to sleep in a bedroom he'd felt sure was haunted. *If I do not see it, it isn't there.*

The corridor the boys eventually emerged in felt different from the rooms below. Liam remembered vaguely that the building had once been a children's home. A long row of cupboards lined the corridor, each one just about big enough for a child to hide in.

Liam couldn't think why this thought had entered his head. It briefly nauseated him but, equally, it seemed to fill his mind, rendering it blank of anything else. As he was about to turn – to tell his friends that enough was enough; they'd reached the pinnacle; they could go back down now – he heard, somewhere to his right, the same peal of laughter he'd heard on the stairs The *same* peal, as if it were not merely the same voice but the precise same moment in time, repeated. Liam had barely processed this before the footsteps sounded, tripping across the floor towards the far wall; and then the penultimate cupboard door slammed.

The boys crowded back against the opposite wall as if as one, then stilled. In daylight hours they played football together and the same group instincts seemed to serve them now. After a second's stunned pause, the boys holding the torches flashed them in the direction of the sound, but of course there was nothing there.

'You all heard that,' Liam said tentatively. 'Didn't you?'

'*No,*' scoffed a friend, 'you're special. Of course we did. It was probably a rat.'

The silence that followed this declaration was clearly dubious. Liam said, 'Go and look in the cupboard, then?'

Another pause. Then the friend said, 'No, what if it bites me? I've had enough. Let's go.'

Liam had no intention of arguing, and nor, it seemed, did anyone else. When the group turned to retrace its steps down the spiral staircase, Liam was sure to insinuate himself into the middle, rather than being forced to bring up the rear. Halfway down he thought he heard again the ripple of children's laughter, but he made himself shut out the sound. It didn't matter. Soon, they would all be home free.

*

Many visitors to Newsham Park have mentioned *the children*. Those who worked there during its time as a psychiatric hospital report that patients often spoke to invisible people – but of course, in a psychiatric institution, this is to be expected. More anxiety-inducing are the tales told by staff about the ominous upper corridor which most feared to enter, having been told its row of cupboards once served as tiny prisons for misbehaving children. Newsham Park's past life as an orphanage seems to have haunted it even in its hospital heyday – but it's true that 16,000 orphans were cremated on the site, their ashes thrown into a pit in the mortuary. If we believe that suffering clings to a place, where else would we expect an infestation than somewhere like Newsham Park, where multiple horrific pasts are layered on top of each other like peeling wallpaper?

'Perhaps "ghost" is just the name we give to a lingering horror,' suggests writer Ella McLeod in a story featured on Richard MacLean Smith's *Unexplained* podcast. McLeod is writing about a house not in the UK but in Jamaica, a former colony still haunted by centuries of slavery. At Rose Hall in Montego Bay, legend has it that the ghost of former mistress Annie Palmer still stalks the grounds. It is said that Annie, Anglo-Irish born, was a voodoo practitioner who married and killed four men, as well as multiple slaves, upon whom she inflicted appalling torture. Ghost hunters and tourists now flock to the crumbling mansion, a monument to Jamaica's brutal past – while locals continue to steer clear of the place, wincing when its name is mentioned.

The thing is, all research indicates that Annie Palmer never existed. The legend appears to derive in large part from various fictional accounts, most notably Herbert G. de Lisser's *The White Witch of Rosehall* (1929). There is no evidence that any of Rose Hall's inhabitants mistreated either their spouses or their slaves – but, they did *keep* slaves, and the horror of that time is stamped onto the landscape in a now indelible way. It doesn't matter whether Annie Palmer really existed, at Rose Hall or elsewhere. The fear of Rose Hall survives, along with our sense of revulsion towards a time long gone but never forgotten. The building may not be haunted by a ghost, as such, but it is peopled with our own direst imaginings, and our guilt about what transpired there.

It is notable that Newsham Park, like Rose Hall, is abandoned. There is something inherently psychologically trying about places that were built for regular occupation and which now stand empty, devoid of the chatter and bustle that once filled them. Anyone who has stumbled across the viral video of Noel Edmonds' brief theme park experiment, 'Crinkley Bottom' or 'Blobbyland' at Cricket St Thomas, will appreciate that the gaudier and more purpose-built the enterprise, the eerier it appears in silent dereliction. Abandoned theme parks have this effect whether or not we imagine anything more sinister than the objectively horrific Mr Blobby ever visited them.

Meanwhile, children's homes and asylums are now deeply embedded in the public imagination: YouTube turns up countless videos of ghost hunters and thrill seekers meandering through the halls of enormous Gothic piles arrested in a time best forgotten. But where the distasteful past of a place has been replaced with something else, we do not find the same tendency to expect hauntings. Strawberry Field, just as gaunt and ominous on the face of it as

Newsham Park, has been imbued with new life, enough to satisfy the restless mind. With Newsham Park, and other places like it, there's a sense that *something* ought to fill this place, built as it was as a hub in which scores of humans lived their daily lives. If there are no new humans – well, then perhaps the unreplaced can never leave.

There's another thing about private places, whether abandoned or not, which doesn't extend to their public counterparts. When we know that an orphanage is abandoned, the sound of a child's laughter can quickly be isolated as an aberration. But in a school, couldn't the laughter of a ghostly child go unobserved? In a school, the occupants are constantly, regularly replaced, and in many ways, replaceable. Isn't it possible that a ghost at the back of the classroom could go unnoticed indefinitely, a child in a place we expect children to be?

This is why, in a public place, a haunting must fit certain criteria in order to register. In the introduction to this book, I talked about Charlie in The Scrogg pub. The barmaids took note of Charlie after hours, but it's entirely possible that he sat unnoticed at the darts table during the day, just another man unremarked amidst the crowd. We expect public places to be filled with people – which is why visiting a school for a parents' evening feels oddly wrong, the classrooms empty and the playground silent. Do ghosts in public places, then, have to pick their moments? Or do we, whether wittingly or not, choose the moments in which we allow ourselves to see them?

Chapter Six
A Public Spectacle

STOP ME IF YOU'VE heard this one.

There used to be a swimming pool on-site, you know.
The girl who carved her initials on the front of your
registration period desk, the boy who inscribed penises
all over your copy of *King Lear* with the dedication of a
medieval monk illuminating a manuscript – they didn't
have to trek to the nearest council swimming baths. They
didn't have to cram into the single branded bus now
used exclusively by the rugby team, or waste the PE
period snaking lugubriously through a housing estate.
There used to be a swimming pool on-site – until
Something Happened there and it was covered over,
never to be used again.

My secondary school had a fictitious swimming pool
whose imagined horrors shifted and flickered through our
lore like shafts of light in water. Specifically, the pool was

said to have been under the canteen, an idea supported
by split-level, hillside construction which meant the ground
floor was some twelve feet up from the actual ground. The
school was opened in 1990 – an academy built on the backs
of two failed comprehensives – and looked more like a car
dealership than anything else. I started there only eight
years later, leaving a vanishingly narrow window of time
in which the grisly event and its subsequent cover-up could
have occurred. This didn't stop us – if anything, the necessary recentness of the event made it more compelling, the
obfuscation more impressive. Somebody had died there,
probably. Sometimes, at night, her ghost could still be seen.
(Nobody had ever seen it, but this lessened our conviction
not one iota.)

The fictitious swimming pool appears to have been a
feature of many schools in the 1990s and 2000s. While
researching this chapter, I heard tell of rumoured subterranean bodies of water in Hull, Stratford, Brighton,
Glasgow and north London. My American partner
recounted her own 'hidden pool' tale from her school in
Albuquerque, New Mexico. In all these cases, the pool
was entirely a product of the collective teenage imagination, its presumed victim merely a logical outgrowth of
the original rumour. I wondered whether the idea had
some traceable root in popular culture – 'Big Fish', a
notoriously egregious 1998 episode of *Buffy the Vampire
Slayer*, sees the Sunnydale High swim team decimated by
a horrific aquatic monster. In *X-Files* episode 'The Walk'
(1995), a female army captain is drowned by a mysterious

creature in an atmospherically dark basement pool. It's possible that these images from popular viewing fare of the time sparked adolescent imaginations; it's equally likely that the idea of the buried pool (and buried scandal) simply taps into many of the tropes common in teenage urban legend. We've talked already about the pull of the underground. The addition of water doubles the sense of an unreachable space, a place not designed for us to live in. Teenage imaginations will routinely produce similar spectres the whole world over, regardless of any real commonality or basis in fact.

At my vast Victorian primary school, the story went that the deep sandstone walls had concealed an air raid shelter during the Second World War. This was not only grossly untrue but also logically flawed: the walls were entirely solid and, indeed, many of our relatives had attended the same school in the 1940s, and could have told us where the shelters really were. But, at an age when the thought of being evacuated to an Anderson Shelter seemed romantic, we didn't want to be corrected. Our uncles and aunts had their own stories, of footsteps in the attic and the unseen hand that sounded the old school bell without warning. Childhood and adolescence are credulous years; at ten, it can be difficult to pinpoint the moment when imagination ends and reality begins.

All the most ubiquitous urban legends derive from this peer group – Bloody Mary; the Hook Man; the burglar who, pretending to be a faithful hound, lies under your bed and licks your hand. Young people seem driven not only to believe, but to reinvent the shared stories which strengthen and sustain their communities. In many ways, these communities are modern echoes of how societies, untroubled by tertiary education and the threat of The Economy, might have behaved in centuries past. No wonder, then, that schools, those pressure-cookers into which we funnel our children to be tempered into acceptable adult beings, are indelibly infused with folklore of their own.

Beyond the social bonding generated by storytelling in our childhood and teenage years, there are other reasons schools might be among the most haunted of our public buildings. Anyone who has dabbled in amateur occultism will have heard the suggestion that children and young people are more susceptible than others to the supernatural – they represent, allegedly, little psychic helipads onto which ghosts might descend. In a school, if both the haunters and the haunted fall within this group, it might be imagined that the likelihood of connection is stronger. Moreover, if you think of yourself at the age of twelve, retreading the long route from PE to French every Friday afternoon for a year, there's something of a spectral aspect to that journey in and of itself. We haunted those corridors; we adhered to those timetables as if our little lives depended on it. In those days, school strictures were our gods. Why should a little thing like death alter that?

Generations of pupils at a primary school in Cardiff seem to agree . . .

A Green Glow

Roath Park Primary, in the north of the city, was opened in 1895 and built in a typically Victorian red brick style employed for similar structures throughout the country. Today it is a well-loved local institution with a boldly cartoonish website whose flashing animations and scrolling text in Comic Sans speak to the lingering presence of the World Wide Web as it was in the year 2000, rather than to any more sinister haunting. Perhaps the reflection it offers is accurate. For decades, Roath Park has been reputedly haunted, but its resident spirit is, by all accounts, a benevolent one.

When Alys secured a role as a teaching assistant at Roath Park, the building was already familiar to her. In the two decades since she attended the school as a pupil herself, its decor had been refreshed, its furniture updated, but the essence of the place remained unchanged. From her new vantage point, Alys recognised all of it: the playground clamour; the way the light fell through the vaulted windows in the late afternoon. The smell of the corridors, that particular school scent of plasticine and PVA glue. And, of course – the ghost.

She had never intended to mention it. As a child, she'd always been aware of the Green Lady, as the being was then commonly known. She remembered flashes of green light glancing off the corners of corridors; once, a jar of pencils upended itself on a teacher's desk, scattering its contents onto the lino. As her schooldays receded into the past, however, Alys became less certain as to what was true memory and what was the afterlife of childish imagination. Children believe in Santa Claus and the Tooth Fairy, in many cases with passionate intensity; to the under-eights, they are entirely real. Alys felt inclined to put the Green Lady – equally benevolent, to her childhood mind – into this category.

The moment she stepped back into the school on a quiet Saturday, she recognised her error.

A school, when inhabited, has an unmistakable energy. The vibrant and even violent emotions of youth reverberate through its walls; a low buzz of laughter and clatter can be heard at a remove, wherever in the building you are. In most schools, this energy dissipates when the children leave. The same cannot be said of Roath Park.

The feeling that greeted Alys that sunny Saturday morning was one that flooded her with instant recognition. There was something so present about it, so vividly alive, that the school felt little different to the way it had the evening before when she'd mistakenly left her phone charger behind before she travelled home. This morning's trip was a flying visit to collect the forgotten item. As Alys ducked into her classroom for it, the sun filtered bright through the high windows. The room was warm, dust motes dancing in the yellow light. The scattered burst of laughter in the corridor – the rushing of footsteps – seemed so in keeping with the scene that Alys barely registered hearing them. Only when she'd locked up and returned to her car did she remember, with a sudden shiver, that the school was empty. The childish sounds must have emerged from the building itself.

Still, as Alys rotated this realisation in her mind on the drive home, she realised she didn't feel frightened. There had always been something in the school, but whatever it was seemed simply an extension of its natural ebullience, something generated and sustained by years of children's play. She'd dismissed it, but now, being close to it again, she had to reconsider. It *was* there. It had always been so.

She didn't raise the idea in the staffroom, even then. Most of the staff were far newer to the school than she was; perhaps without the underlying context of having been a pupil here, the presence at the school was less readily detectable. Since that Saturday, Alys had become more attuned to it, catching the echoes of footsteps in empty halls when the children were all outside in the yard, or the *snick* of a door being closed by some unseen hand. But the thought of mentioning it made her queasy. She couldn't imagine the parents of the twenty-first century taking kindly to such concepts being placed in their children's heads.

One morning break, another teacher came into the staffroom smiling wryly as she deposited her handbag on the sofa and reached for the solace of the kettle. 'The Green Man's been at it again this morning,' she remarked.

'Again?'

Alys was glad someone else had responded so she needn't betray her interest, but she *was* interested, deeply so. The teacher, peeling the foil off the top of a new jar of Nescafé, seemed far less perturbed.

'The usual,' she said. 'Kids at the back of the class making a fuss about it – "Who's that green man?" I said he was my TA.'

The pair laughed. The atmosphere in the room did not shift. Alys thought of the flashes of green she recalled from her childhood at the school, and wondered.

*

The green man, woman, or non-binary entity of Roath Park Primary has been the subject of rumours for years. A recent WalesOnline article attests to its longevity: another former pupil-turned-teaching assistant, Chris Webber, recalls having heard of the friendly spectre as a child and now wonders whether it 'roams the extensive attics'. Again, the allure of the school's inaccessible spaces insinuates itself into the narrative – but the first-hand stories of the entity depict it much closer to the heart of operations.

An administrative manager complained that the spectre 'trips the phones', describing it as a 'friendly energy' of indeterminate gender. One long-serving teacher describes having witnessed doors slamming, lights being flicked on and off, and various objects flung from tables. The green element of the spectre, interestingly enough, seems confined to children's visions, with pupils having signalled the presence of a green being in the classroom on repeated occasions. One five-year-old described the entity as being 'green, no hair. Friendly'.

Those associated with the school have attempted to draw connections between the green colour and the ghost's potential provenance. The enduring national preoccupation with the Second World War perhaps inevitably raises its head here: could the green be that of an army uniform, a teacher killed in action? Another suggestion is that the green reflects the colour of a dinner lady's uniform, a benevolent figure still attending to her duties in the afterlife. It's notable that the most traditional associations with green no longer seem to leap readily to mind. Green has, at times, been the colour of witches. More commonly it has been associated with the Fair Folk: fairies are often described as either being or wearing green in British folklore, with, for example, one Scots Gaelic song depicting them as '*luchd nan trasganan uaine*', the tribe of the green mantles. Today, we no longer expect to see the green glimpse of a fairy. However, it seems there are times when we see the flash of green all the same, and struggle to connect it to a concept which makes more contextual sense to the world we are living in. Green for a soldier or green for a fairy – either way, the green remains.

It's an interesting thought. Like the modern-day miners who translated blue lights and clattering underground into the work of spirits, rather than the fairies and goblins in which their predecessors believed, the green entity of Roath Park shows a long-recorded phenomenon being refitted into a form more readily understandable to its witnesses today. And, as in many tales, it's children to whom the being itself is actually visible, while adults seem to perceive it only through its physical interactions with the world. A leap of faith has to be made here, of course – who is to say that the green presence, 'friendly' with the children, is behind the low-level poltergeist activity adults have experienced? Or that, if it is, its intentions towards those past school age are not of a more sinister kind?

The being has never committed any serious acts of violence. Safer, then, to believe in its benevolence, especially if it could be your uncanny co-worker for years to come.

*

Of the Roath Park spectre, one teacher, Mike, observed to WalesOnline: 'It's our ghost. So many teachers and children have been through the school it's not surprising some would like to pop back [as a ghost].'

This rather endearing idea of 'popping back' to a place once well-loved in life is particularly common to hauntings in public places. Many public ghosts, like the green glow of Roath Park Primary, manifest as something between lawful neutral and chaotic good. Footsteps – like those heard in The Scrogg – are an incredibly common type of haunting, as if a previous visitor's path were so regularly trodden that it left its mark not only on a building's floorboards and flagstones, but in its very atmosphere. Some spectres interact more directly with the modern world, as when the green ghost of Roath Park sends pen pots and picture books flying. In few cases, though, is the spirit of a still-functioning public building actively *malevolent*. This makes a certain kind of sense – after all, a space beset by spiritual pests might struggle to remain attractive to the public for long.

In the modern era, many places afflicted by such infestations have closed their doors to their original clientele and opened instead as monuments to their own insidious reputations: psychiatric institutions, schools and public houses up and down the country now pay their way as ghosts of their former selves, home to psychic walks and spectral vigils. Ghost business, in its own way, is big business – but it isn't *daily* business. In order to be an acceptable public ghost, a spirit mustn't make too much of a nuisance of itself. Poltergeist activity is one thing when you've paid your entrance fee in the keen hope of witnessing it; it's quite another to be interrupted by rattling tables and raps on the wall when you're trying to slog through your GCSEs.

Schools represent a snapshot universe of our childhood and adolescent years, brimming with memories repeatedly overlaid upon one another until they achieve a kind of permanence. For most of us, though, there are other places which become fixtures in our adult lives just as our institutions of learning were in the years before. Places of work are one example – like schools, many shops and offices feel somehow removed from themselves when entered out of hours, the fabric of the building taut like a breath inhaled and held. Unlike schools, however, many work-places do not adhere to a pattern of daytime use only.

The Department of Social Security in Long Benton in North Tyneside, for example, functioned on strange shift patterns for years, with night-shift workers keeping watch over the computers which sustained HMRC's processes and which, in the 1970s and '80s, often occupied whole rooms. In the North-East, the DSS is a significant employer, and more than one former shift worker attested to odd experiences in the building at night – as when computer operator Rodney entered what he thought was an empty room to find a man lying prone on a conference table. Baffled, he asked whether the figure needed help, then ventured back out of the room to ask a colleague whether anybody else was supposed to be on shift with them. Had someone fallen ill on an earlier shift and been forgotten? When he returned to the room and switched on the light, there was nobody there. The incongruity of the experience sent a prickle down Rodney's spine – after so many years of use, he thought, countless people had probably died in the building and perhaps had been laid out like that, waiting for help that didn't come fast enough. But, he said, he couldn't be sure. During a night shift, there were always people wandering around, taking an hour's break in a quiet place, hoping not to be seen. And, in such a huge institution, it was no surprise to encounter a person once and never again. Rodney had a 'bad feeling' about the figure on the table which has stayed with him for years, but he admits to the possibility of the man having leaped up and made a swift exit unnoticed by Rodney and his pal. The DSS works all hours.

The same is true of many law firms, where several junior associates have reported seeing strange shadows moving in the small hours of the morning – but where they themselves have regularly spent whole nights, working towards important trials in an industry that dares not sleep.

'I was sure there was somebody there with me,' said one young lawyer, Prita, who is convinced she once saw a humanoid shadow drift slowly along a silent corridor, pass the door of her office and then disappear. 'But maybe it really was just *someone*? I was there at 2 a.m., after all. Someone else might have been.'

The tales of office hauntings I was told often fitted this pattern – and, compared to the numerous stories of alleged school spectres, the stories were few. While offices occupy a significant proportion of our adult lives, our lives there lack the inevitable rigidity of our schooldays, when we arrive and leave at fixed times which may be deviated from only for certain, specifically defined reasons. The professional, no-nonsense personae we tend to project while at work may also have something to do with the 'hedging' element common to many of these recollections. One woman, a project manager at an insurance company, recalled hearing a distinct cough in an empty office one Sunday morning – the cough set her on edge, but it was the subsequent coincidental clatter of a crow slamming into the window which put her in a state of panic. The unexpected cough primed her; the crash had her bolting from the office, sure that the eerie human sound had somehow presaged the collision. Afterwards, she unpicked her thoughts: perhaps there had, after all, been another person in the office? Of course, the coincidence was only that, and nothing more. She couldn't be sure. The professional skin she wore to work in that office was not the sort of person who'd say for certain that she'd spent the morning with a ghost.

Not all of us, however, work in offices. As a teenager, I had a job in a branch of Staples which was glamorous only in that it paid its under-eighteens the adult minimum wage. Everybody else on the Saturday staff was below the age of twenty, creating a somewhat anarchic *Lord of the Flies* environment in which it often felt that nobody knew the rules. As I skulked through the dark, lofty, silent storerooms replenishing stock on my own, I regularly thought the place felt as if it could be haunted. It wasn't – but apparently, there are lots of retail outlets whose most inconvenient regulars are denizens of the spirit world, particularly when the lawless teenage weekend crew is in charge.

The Bootmakers'

Between 2018 and 2019, Sophie – then ploughing through her sixth-form years – worked Thursday evenings and Saturdays at a shoe shop in Canterbury. Sandwiched between a betting shop and what can only be described as a purveyor of random tat, the smart-fronted emporium, set in a relatively modern brick arcade, appeared utterly innocuous. Sophie had no great ambitions in the shoe trade; perhaps she'd have preferred Accessorize, but a shoe shop was several cuts above the fast food restaurants where many of her friends spent their evenings. At least she wouldn't come home reeking of grease. This was the sort of job, she thought, where you could leave your work at work.

What she found was somewhat to the contrary.

This was Sophie's first job, and she meant to do it well. For the first week or two, she keenly shadowed the manager, Simon, as he explained how to log in to the till; how to process a sale; how to issue a refund. When it was time to fetch a pair of shoes for a customer, he led her up the creaking stairs to the stockroom on the first floor, past the row of slightly dilapidated lockers where the staff left their personal items during shifts.

'They're organised by size,' he explained, 'and then by type, so . . .'

Sophie took notes as he talked, knowing that soon she would be serving customers alone. This wasn't the sort of shoe shop where everything is lined up on the rails; if a gentleman wanted the display boot in a size twelve, it would need to be retrieved from the storeroom. So, Sophie strove to memorise the system, noting where boots gave way to shoes and men's to ladies'. The stockroom itself made little impression on her, beyond the fact that the upper corners needed dusting.

When the pair returned to the shop floor, Sophie took up her position on the till as instructed. While she was logging in, her colleague, Olivia – another teenage girl – elbowed her in the side and smiled. 'What did you think of the stockroom?'

Sophie was puzzled. 'What do you mean?'

'You'll see,' said Olivia, with an enigmatic raise of the brow; and then, unable to resist, added: 'It's haunted.'

'Oh,' Sophie said, thinking she was beginning to understand. 'Haunted, is it? OK. I'll keep an eye out.'

Olivia maintained an expression of impressive composure. 'You do that,' she said.

By the following Saturday, Sophie had been ruled fit to serve alone, with the reassurance of a lapel pin which declared 'I'm New!' in the appropriate brand font. Her first customer wanted a boot that would have to be fetched from upstairs, as Sophie had expected. As she headed up the creaking stairs, however, she reminded herself to expect something else. 'Haunted stockroom' was evidently an initiation ritual of sorts. Probably there was someone waiting upstairs to lunge out from behind a stack of boxes, or emit a menacing groan from the darkness of the cupboard. Sophie was determined to be on her guard – it wouldn't do to show weakness.

The name and size of the desired boot was scrawled on a scrap of paper in Sophie's hand, and she referred to this as she made her way carefully around the room, checking labels. It might have been rather a soothing task in its mundanity, but Sophie's body was on high alert. Between each step, she paused to listen, not wanting the rustling of her clothes or the sound of her breathing to drown out any telltale noises. She moved, and moved again, and there seemed to be nobody there; but the staff was half composed of teenage boys, and Sophie *knew* teenage boys. When she reached the correct boot and pulled the box from the shelf without incident, she actually wondered if something had gone wrong. Then—

Click.

Sophie didn't recognise the sound at first. The slow creaking that followed gave it away: the door, which she'd firmly closed, swinging open. Despite herself, a shiver skittered across the back of her neck. She'd been on the alert for brash boyish japes and daftness. This sort of subtlety was definitely worse; she had to privately applaud them.

Aloud, she said, 'Oh, very funny. Is that all you've got?'

Silence. Sophie huffed, hefted the box more comfortably into her arms and headed for the stairs. Only as she was going down them, lamenting the way they groaned and protested under every step, did the thought crawl warily across her mind that she hadn't heard a sound to indicate descent after the door had been opened.

The customer was waiting, glancing impatiently at her watch, which in its own way was a blessing. Sophie opened the box; admired the boots when the customer tried them on; and ran through the patter about polish and leather care kits as she walked the woman to the till. When the sale was completed, the manager made a point of congratulating her on how she'd handled it, and Sophie let the glow push the uncertainty out of her mind. Later, on the bus home, she let herself mull it all over. Perhaps the latch was loose? There might never have been a prank in the offing, after all. A door that eerily opened on its own could be enough, Sophie thought, to give a lonely stockroom a reputation.

Next time, she thought, she would pay it no mind.

For some months, Sophie succeeded in this resolution. She was good at her job, she found; she had a natural rapport with the customers and was popular with her colleagues. When they mentioned the haunted stockroom, she would laugh along – especially when someone scuttled white-faced down the stairs, clearly perturbed by what Sophie felt could only be a wonky latch and an uneven floorboard. It was all right to join in; it was part of the camaraderie of their little enterprise. And, when the door happened to click out of place when Sophie was upstairs alone, it made her heart catch, but she knew – she was sure – it was innocent. There was nothing to be worried about.

September was always a turning point, or, as Simon put it, 'a churning point'. Two members of staff were leaving Canterbury to take up university places, which left Olivia and Sophie as senior members of the weekend team. One evening, soon after school had started again, Simon asked Sophie to help him lock up.

'It's just tidying up after the others have gone,' he explained, 'and they like to have two of us here. It's policy. You'd get a little bonus for it.'

Sophie, currently saving for university herself, was not about to turn down any kind of raise.

In the event, it was all very easy. Olivia and Dan, the new boy, left. Simon headed upstairs for a final sweep of the stockroom, leaving Sophie to tidy up any remaining detritus in the shop below. There wasn't much. She tucked loose tissue paper into the wastepaper basket and sang to herself under her breath as she worked. She heard the stairs creak in a familiar way as Simon ascended.

The next sound was less familiar. As Sophie leaned down to pick up a discarded shoebox from the shop floor, a sudden metallic clamour made her freeze in place. It was like doors clanging shut: not one, or two, but several doors, as if slammed in sequence. Sophie felt suddenly unable to move. After a long moment, she found her voice.

'Simon?' she croaked. It wasn't loud enough for him to hear from upstairs. She cleared her throat and tried again. 'Simon!'

Footsteps clattered down the stairs and Sophie straightened in relief to see – nothing. Transfixed, she stood in place as the steps hurtled towards the front door of the shop, and then ceased as if they had never been.

A moment later, Simon materialised on the stairs, looking white and shaken. 'Were you up here?' he asked weakly. 'Messing about with the lockers?'

'No,' Sophie said, her voice a sliver of a thing.

'I heard you run down the stairs,' Simon said.

'I heard it too,' Sophie admitted. 'It wasn't me.'

After a second's pause, Simon seemed to collect himself. He sloped down the stairs and towards the till. As if mechanically, he logged off. While the computer was shutting down, he said, 'It's done it before. Hey, don't – leave, all right? It never gets any worse than this.'

'All right,' Sophie promised obediently. 'If it doesn't get worse.'

She only had to make it to the next 'churning point', after all. This was what powered her through the Thursday closings, the winter Saturday mornings when the street was still dark as they unlocked the doors. A footstep here, a door slammed there. Sophie decided she could handle it, knowing there was an end in sight. How Simon managed it, she never understood.

*

Beyond the world of work, there are other places which many of us haunt in our adult lives, and where professional standards do not inhibit or protect us. The introduction to this book described a public house haunting with which I have long been familiar; when soliciting ghost stories, the 'haunted pub' trope was one which recurred repeatedly, without any of the 'perhaps' attached to workplace wonderings. In considering public ghosts, then, it seems fitting to examine some of the spectral residue attributed to public houses, where potent spirits of all kinds apparently mix.

*

I came by this story completely by chance. For that reason, it's one of my favourites. I hadn't asked about ghosts when it was told to me. I hadn't mentioned my quest for evidence of modern-day paranormal belief in the UK. On the contrary, I was off the clock, and hoping to be more so. I had asked about a roadside pub which I regularly pass on my travels through the wilds of Oxfordshire. Once or twice, I'd considered stopping, but its location always seemed rather odd to me – stranded in an agricultural hinterland between towns, a B-road on one side and a canal, complete with roosting longboats, on the other. Was it a nice pub, I asked the office at large. Would anyone recommend it?

'The garden's nice,' said a colleague, who'd lived in the area all her life. 'They've just got a new chef; I keep meaning to try him out. A friend of mine's parents used to have that pub. It's haunted.'

My contemplation of the pub's extensive menu was immediately arrested by this revelation. I pressed: 'Haunted?'

'Yes,' said my colleague, 'by a man.' She laughed, suddenly sheepish. Her office persona, perhaps, should be more sceptical.

I ignored the sheepishness. 'Tell me about it,' I said.

Old Haunts

Karen's parents bought the pub in 1995. I was asked not to give its name, but suffice it to say it is an old, but not ancient, building, dating from the late-eighteenth century and in continual use as a public house since the early twentieth. Its location, in a village so small it is accessed via a single-track road signposted '[VILLAGE NAME] Only', belies the level of trade it attracts from two directions: on one side, the main thoroughfare to Oxford; and on the other, the canal which remains a busy waterway, even in 2024. Before I visited, I searched its name and was enticed by a TripAdvisor review which suggested I 'AVOID THIS PLACE AT ALL COSTS' – but, disappointingly, the aggrieved reviewer simply wished to complain about his pie. '[Pub Name] Haunted' returns no results. In pre-internet days, it would have been even more difficult for Karen's parents to hear that the pub might have a pre-existing resident when they moved in. Still, my colleague assured me, if you're local, you know.

The first experience Karen had of the haunting was, as seems often to be the case, the sound of footsteps. The pub is long and low, consisting of several rooms connected in some cases by doors, in others by archways where a door might once have hung. A spiral staircase at one end leads up to the first-floor rooms inhabited by the landlord's family. Karen's bedroom was at the top of these stairs. There was a bathroom for family use on the upper floor, as well as a sitting area and a small kitchenette. After closing time – once the family had cleaned up and retired upstairs – there was no reason for anyone to descend the stairs again until morning. Naturally, then, Karen was somewhat confused to be awoken after midnight by heavy footsteps ascending.

Above all, it was the direction of travel which worried her most. There were only three people, to her knowledge, in the pub: herself, her father, and her diminutive mother. The footsteps suggested a man's weight, something firmer and heavier than Karen's mother would be capable of producing, but Karen's father was still asleep. She knew this as anyone for some significant radius around would have known it – because of his snoring. Karen had lived with the sound so long that it was almost soothing to her, a signal that it was time to sleep. On this night, though, as the footsteps passed her door, the familiar sawing noise filled her with fear. Nobody had gone *down* into the pub from the upper storey – of this she was certain. That could only mean that a stranger was coming *up*.

Although she had an office job, she'd pitched in to help her mother behind the bar from seven o'clock to closing time, watching the regulars get more and more unsteady on their feet. Karen didn't drink on duty, but now she wished she'd poured herself a nightcap, the better to sleep through this racket. If she was going to be killed in her bed, she'd rather not know about it. It wasn't as if she was going to open the door. That was absolutely out of the question.

At the top of the stairs was a narrow corridor which ran the length of the pub. All the upstairs rooms branched off it: her parents' room; the bathroom; the sitting area. Its Grade II-listed floorboards were sunken in the middle and creaked reassuringly underfoot. Karen had lived here long enough to be familiar with the transition from stairway tread to corridor, a solid thumping that yielded to a gentler but persistent whine. All the way up the stairs, the footsteps thumped. When they reached the landing, they stopped dead.

Karen held her breath and listened, but she knew that however loudly the blood might be rushing in her ears, it would not cover the creak of the floorboards if there was someone walking across them. After some time, she let herself exhale fully. The pub remained completely silent. If somebody was really waiting on the landing to kill them all, he must have the poise of a ballet dancer to hold so still.

Eventually, Karen forced herself to open the bedroom door, then switched on the light. The staircase was flooded instantly with a sterile glow from the bare bulb above. Of course, as she'd known it would be, it was empty. But the thump of feet on the stairs still echoed in her head, deliberate and unmistakable. Someone had been here. The question was – who?

The following morning, Karen asked her parents whether anyone had gone back downstairs after closing time. She already knew the answer, but nevertheless, their denials made her stomach dip uncomfortably. A snatch of old verse entered her head – *Yesterday, upon the stair, I met a man who wasn't there.* Like the poet (William Hughes Mearns) she hoped he'd go away, but had little faith in her wish being granted.

Mearns's well-known poem, 'Antigonish', tells the story of a spirit which reputedly roamed the halls of a house in Antigonish, Nova Scotia. In it, the speaker implores the unwelcome visitor to leave – but 'please don't slam the door!' Perhaps the lurker in the pub had been inspired by it. At any rate, after several instances of unauthorised stair-climbing, door-slamming was its next volley. Karen's nocturnal visitor, however, seemed to have an advantage over Mearns's. In Mearns's poem, it's only the little man who isn't there. In Karen's case, it was not only the man, but the door as well.

The pub's original build, with heavy doors connecting a series of smaller rooms, had probably been intended to keep the heat in, but that had been in the days when pubs served only drinks and whatever stew was currently on the go. For a waitress carrying a heavily laden tray from kitchen to customer, multiple doors would have presented an obstacle – which is why, Karen assumed, most of them had been removed. A heavy oak door remained at either end of the building, but the intervening archways now stood empty, only the lintels indicating they had once been occupied. The doors that remained were far too heavy to be moved by even the strongest of winds; indeed, they had both swollen with age, the pub's position on the water making it susceptible to damp. When they were closed at night, they scraped noticeably across the flagstones beneath. So, when Karen was setting a round of plates onto a table in a central room, it startled not only her but everyone present when a door slammed violently behind her.

Her natural inclination was to freeze. When she recovered herself, she managed to apologise, suggesting that someone must have slammed the external door.

'No,' said one of the diners, gesturing, 'it's still open – look.'

It was.

'Don't worry,' the diner said, although he looked slightly grey. 'He does this sometimes. Can't be helped.'

Karen didn't ask who 'he' might be. She didn't want to know. If the answer was 'the ghost that lives here', she thought she knew quite enough about him already.

As time went on, Karen realised that the aural hauntings, the steps on the stair and the slamming of the absent door, were regular occurrences. Not *frequently,* but on multiple occasions, she heard the familiar patterns of sound occur without warning. Her mother had witnessed the door-slamming, too, but the pair rarely spoke about it. Karen decided that the sounds were, in their own way, recordings, impressions of a person, but not evidence of a sentient being as such. The footsteps, she thought, were a sound like any other noise a house might make when it settled. The idea comforted her. Sounds alone never hurt anybody.

One evening in June, Karen was behind the bar with her mother, serving the final regulars after the bell for last orders had rung. By now a finely oiled team, the pair pulled pints and took change, until the patrons had filtered back to their tables to down their last beers at speed. They had begun wiping down the bar when Karen saw her father appear in the doorway, gesturing.

Karen stopped and wrinkled her nose, confused. Her father was motioning towards the bar, and Karen held up the cloth as if to indicate: *I'm sorting it!* Eventually, her

250

father shook his head in some frustration and strode towards the end of the bar, leaning his weight on it to speak directly into Karen's ear.

'Aren't you going to serve him?' he said. 'He was waiting in good time.'

Karen stilled, as did her mother beside her. The two women looked at each other, and then at the land-lord with a growing sense not so much of fear as of resignation.

One of them had to say it. 'Who?' asked Karen's mother warily.

Karen's father frowned and indicated the empty bar.

'There's nobody there, Dad,' said Karen gently.

Karen's father looked up and his face drained instantly of colour. He had never heard the footsteps, or the slammings. Whenever the sounds had been briefly mentioned, he had always found a way to change the subject. But the man who wasn't there had found his way to him just the same.

*

The ghost of the canalside pub has always been incred-ibly predictable in his behaviours. After the incident with the disappearing figure, Karen decided to ask around, only to hear from regular customers that his presence had been remarked upon for decades. She observed that there wasn't much evidence of the haunting further afield, whereupon a daily bar-propper pointed out, 'Well, he doesn't do much, does he? He's just here, same as the rest of us.'

Karen's belief that the pub hauntings are simply recordings echoes the 'Stone Tape Theory', with which many of us will be familiar, whether by name or not. In a way, it's rather a commonsense idea, working in the realms of the metaphysical but not quite the supernatural. Stone Tape Theory suggests that hauntings are similar to tape recordings, the energy deriving from emotional or traumatic events somehow having inscribed itself onto buildings and other items which then retain it and 'replay' it.

The idea has its roots in the nineteenth century. Charles Babbage's *Ninth Bridgewater Treatise* (1837) suggests that words spoken aloud might have the capacity to leave indelible impressions in the atmosphere, connected in some fashion to the way motion is transferred between particles. During the heights of spiritualist fervour in the late nineteenth and early twentieth centuries, the Society for Psychical Research espoused the similar idea of 'place memory', although in their view, a 'recording' could be accessed only by a gifted individual or psychic medium. Useful, naturally, when one is seeking to explain why a ghost is present but only special people can see or hear it.

Stone Tape Theory has been widely dismissed in recent years as pseudoscientific and irrational, particularly given its connections to psychometry, the idea that a so-called 'cold reading' can be conducted by handling an object imbued with the energy of a deceased person.

However, this didn't stop it becoming popularised in the twentieth century, with a 1972 BBC television play, *The Stone Tape*, bringing it to widespread attention. Scientists and philosophers might lament the propagation of a theory with no real basis in fact – in this case, they certainly do. Theodore Schick and Lewis Vaughn, in their book *How to Think About Weird Things: Critical Thinking for a New Age* (2013), decried the prevalence of the idea, observing accurately that 'chunks of stone just do not have the same properties as reels of tape'. Self-evidently not – but the trouble is, to the untrained person, the concept of Stone Tape Theory *seems* to make decent sense as an explanation for the otherwise unexplainable. When we have heard the footsteps, or witnessed the figure, or watched the door slam, a theory which *seems* to make sense can have a fatal attraction for us.

Many of those who first espoused Stone Tape Theory hoped it could explain all types of ghosts, but many modern believers seem to place experiences into two categories: those that are recordings – repetitive, predictable, and interacting only with the long-standing physical environment – and those that aren't. A significant majority of pub ghosts seem to fit into the former category, with some of the 'recordings' being far older than others. At the George and Dragon pub in Chester, built above an old Roman road, the drum of marching feet is often heard beneath the floors, with the sound being most evident in the cellars, once the original road level. There have been reports of an occasional Roman soldier sighted above ground, too.

The Lion and Snake in Lincoln suffers from a similar subterranean affliction of centurions – but also boasts an unassuming spectral drinker, whose only misbehaviour is that he tends to get up and dissolve into the wall at the end of the night. At Lendal Cellars in York, the hooded figures of friars are occasionally witnessed by drinkers – apposite, given that the pub is sited where a medieval friary once stood, before its destruction during the Reformation. Meanwhile, at the Bear Hotel in Havant, a woman is reported to walk the corridor by night, audibly toying with her vast collection of keys. The Druid's Head in Brighton boasts a woman in red who waits at the bar, but never stays long enough to be served.

Hauntings of this sort are an accepted part of the environment in many popular watering holes, like fruit machines and the ubiquitous jukebox that does not acknowledge any year after 1985. More alarming – but also more infrequent – are the active pests, the poltergeists, the presences whose actions seem to eerily imply a thinking consciousness. At The Chequers in Bromley, such a presence is said to have knocked a visitor bodily to the floor. In The Ship, in Exeter, a barman was violently pushed, narrowly avoiding an unwanted trip down the stairs. And the Ancient Ram Inn in Wotton under Edge, near Bristol, has been so plagued by supposedly occult forces that its tenure as a public house has now, after almost eight centuries, ended. Its former owner, John Humphries, claimed to have been regularly attacked by demonic entities within the house, while the skeletal remains of children were uncovered beneath the staircase. The pub, which once supposedly sequestered an accused witch, has since been featured on numerous television programmes and can be hired by would-be ghost hunters for 'sleepovers'. Its dark reputation has quite literally pushed it to a change of career – and it's a testament to our continued fascination with ghosts that this has been possible.

Most public places, however, are able to retain their original functions, even where previous users of the facilities seem disinclined to leave. It's notable, too, that so few of the regularly spotted apparitions in Britain's pubs seem to betray any evidence of the trauma once thought necessary for a 'Stone Tape' recording to be made. On the contrary: the stair-climbers, door-slammers and bar-proppers are simply going about their business alongside the living clientele, as if unwilling to admit the party's over. Often, what betrays them is only the tiniest indication of having failed to keep up with the times – perhaps the clothing is outdated, or there is, unfortunately, no longer a door to slam. Sometimes, as in school hauntings, it's simply a matter of timing: when a pub is closed to the living public, the presence of a deceased guest stands out.

There are some public places – few, but some – that never close. Hospitals, nursing homes – how do we distinguish the living from the dead in places like this, especially when the boundary between the two states is perhaps thinner here than anywhere else? How do we know who's lingered too long? Is it even possible?

Night Shift

In the early 2000s, Andrea was a newly qualified nurse working at a former convent hospital in greater Belfast. The building was old, but not remarkably so. Its cheerful red brick edifice reflected its original use as a private home; only in the late nineteenth century had it been purchased by an enterprising group of nuns intent on founding a hospital. Andrea knew this, as everyone did, from her training, and because she had grown up locally. Convent hospitals in Northern Ireland are easy to come by.

So, too, are hospital ghost stories. Nursing, like military service, is a profession entwined far more closely than others with the minutiae of life and death. Becoming a nurse, like becoming a soldier, involves long hours often worked at night, with the knowledge that mutual trust is of vital importance and any mistake could be fatal. When she joined the night shift at the convent hospital, Andrea felt her mettle was being tested. As she arrived at the nurses' station after a long walk through the dimly lit ward, a fellow nurse would often ask, 'Did you see the nun on your way in?'

Andrea always laughed, as she was meant to, but the thought made her uneasy. One of the senior nurses had once described, straight-faced, having locked eyes with a nun who crossed her in the corridor and then, quite abruptly, disappeared. Officially there were no longer any nuns in the hospital, but the senior nurse, a woman with twenty years' experience, disagreed. The straightforwardness of her conviction was enough to unsettle Andrea as she moved about the ward at night, turning off lights and attending to patients' calls. She never saw the nun, but in the perpetual twilight of the hospital, amid the gentle susurrating humming of machinery, she often felt she might. Suggestion is a powerful thing in the small hours.

One night, about six months into her tenure at the hospital, Andrea was seated with a colleague at the nurses' station on the Cardiology ward. The vast majority of patients on the ward were elderly: some awaiting surgery, others recovering from it, and a few being monitored for chronic conditions. Less acutely ill patients were assigned to a central block of beds in the open part of the ward, while others, particularly the high-risk and long-stayers, inhabited private rooms around the periphery. Each patient was equipped with a button which, when pressed, would send an alarm to the nurses' station. By this time in the morning, the lights were all off unless someone needed help. Andrea and her colleague each had a low reading lamp, and the nurses' station was a softly illuminated island in the darkness.

It's a curious thing that the human eye will adjust more quickly to almost-total darkness than to an irregular pattern of light. Although Andrea's reading lamp was low, it still made the wider darkness freshly startling every time she looked up from her paperwork. The stark green glow of the fire exit door, the sudden blare of light when a patient turned on the overhead to shuffle to the toilet – every flash was like a beacon. This was why, when a light suddenly clicked on in one of the side rooms, Andrea noticed it at once.

She elbowed her colleague. 'Room nine?'

The colleague, an older woman with neat fair hair, furrowed her brow. 'Room nine's just had open heart surgery. He hasn't pressed his button?'

'No,' Andrea said, 'but his light's on.'

The other nurse raised her head in confusion. 'It's not,' she pointed out.

Andrea blinked. It wasn't.

For a moment the two of them sat in tense silence – Andrea torn between the anxiety that her mind was going, and the fear of being the butt of a developing practical joke. But the colleague was not the joking type, and the Cardiology ward would never have been the place for japes, even among trainees. As the two looked into the darkness and Andrea considered what to say, the light in room nine flashed on again.

'Oh!' The other nurse sounded alarmed, and Andrea was almost as relieved as she was baffled not to be thought a liar.

'That's the second time,' she said, 'and he's—'

Off went the light, plunging that quarter of the ward back into darkness. A pause, and then it surged on again. The spaces between the toggles of the switch were decreasing, like the space between thunderclaps.

The other nurse stood up. 'He shouldn't be out of his bed,' she said, but her voice was uncertain. 'Let's go and check on him.'

Off–on, went the light. *Off–on–off.* Andrea felt frozen in place. 'It could be the electrics?'

The other nurse gave her a flat look. Of course, it *could* have been the electrics, but they'd never forgive themselves if it wasn't.

The short journey across the ward was more disorienting than Andrea had ever known it, the flickering of the light making it impossible to get a grasp on the shapes in the darkness. As they neared room nine, however, the rising beeping of the heart monitor overrode such concerns. The beeping was cresting – cresting – and as Andrea opened the door, the beeping became a sustained wail. The patient was descending into cardiac arrest.

The light clicked on again, and stayed that way.

The next few minutes were a frantic blur of activity. The code was paged, the crash cart called, and by the time it arrived, Andrea and her colleague were already hard at work with the defibrillators. As the team worked, fluorescent light blazed out through the windows of room nine into the ward beyond, and by the time the patient was stabilised there was daylight filtering in. Andrea's shift was coming to an eventful end just as the world beyond the ward began to stir again, the first buses puttering past and the early commuters setting out. As always after an incident, she felt exhausted. She and her colleague packed their things and left the hospital in near silence, the strange incident with the lights pushed out of their minds by all the subsequent drama.

The next day, Andrea arrived for her shift in the early evening. As she passed room nine on the way in, she opened the door to see how its occupant was faring.

'You gave us a scare yesterday,' she told him as she flipped through his chart to check for any recent interventions.

In the bed, the patient laughed. '*You* were scared? I could feel it all going wrong.'

'But you couldn't press the call button?' Andrea asked, suddenly wary. The light was fading outside and the memory of the curious flickering, banished by stress and daylight, was surging back to her.

The patient looked at her consideringly. 'It was the light that brought you over, wasn't it? I've been telling the other nurse, there was some mad woman flicking it on and off. And thank God, too.'

Andrea's stomach dropped. 'A woman?'

'Yes,' said the patient. 'Must've been wandering about. You surely saw her on her way out? I was a bit preoccupied, myself.'

'Yes,' said Andrea faintly. She couldn't bring herself to tell the truth. She thought of her colleague, and the nun, and their locked eyes, and felt cold all over – but at least she hadn't had to see this woman herself. Thank God indeed for that.

'Lucky coincidences,' said the patient.

*

It's no surprise that hospitals – strange microcosms of their own where there are no after-hours and where life and death hang daily in the balance – are among some of our most haunted public places. What is surprising, perhaps, is that so many reported hospital hauntings adhere to a pattern so predictable that it has its own name, in the nursing profession and beyond. The haunting Andrea recounted is a modern example of the 'Grey Nurse' phenomenon which has been reported in hospitals the world over. Notably, most of those who report seeing such apparitions are nurses themselves.

There's good reason for that, particularly when we consider the idea that a public ghost has to be *noticed*. In a pub or school, this may be because the apparition seems out of time, in terms of its after-hours presence in the building or the way it interacts with its surroundings. In a hospital, however, we can expect to pass almost anyone in a corridor at any time of the day or night – if we're only visiting. It's the nurses who will notice an extra pair of hands on the shift, a light switched on in an unoccupied room. Recent years have reinforced more than ever that nurses are the backbone of the National Health Service: many of them, it seems, are unwilling to abandon their rounds even after the minor inconvenience of their own deaths.

Grey Nurses come in many forms, apparently date from many eras, and have made their presence felt in hospitals across the world. Passing apparitions, like the nun Andrea's colleague reported seeing, skirt the edge of the

phenomenon, but they are not strictly part of it. A Grey
Nurse, fundamentally, is more than a benevolent apparition. She is active, at work, on call. Grey Nurses activate
patients' buzzers when they cannot do the job themselves;
they empty bedpans so the harried nurse on shift doesn't
have to. Multiple nurses have reported being asked by
patients to pass on their thanks to a kind colleague – who
certainly was not on the duty roster. The Royal Adelaide
Hospital in South Australia has a particularly famous
spectre whose favourite trick is to coax patients to sleep
when their pain medication has lost its efficacy. Modern-day
nurses might well be flustered by their interactions with
these silent sisters, but a key commonality among Grey
Nurses is that they are essentially angels of mercy, even
when they seem to be harbingers of death.

The presence of ghost stories as one of the pillars of
nursing culture has been remarked upon by many. Just as
those who spend their lives below ground, in coal mines
and tunnels, develop a tight-knit community where the
dead still play their part, so do many nurses feel a bond
with colleagues both living and dead. Claire Laurent, a
former clinical nurse, considered the role of ghost stories
in the profession in her 2019 book, *Myths and Rituals in
Nursing: A Social History.*

When she trained, Laurent said, 'stories about ghosts
were very strong. Everyone just accepted them, whether
they believed in ghosts or not.' She adds that 'no one was
scared by them, even though some of the stories were
quite horrific.' Instead, Laurent found from her research

that most believed the apparitions served a functional purpose, with some offering warnings that stopped over-tired nurses from administering the wrong medication. Speaking to the industry magazine *Nursing Standard*, one nurse, Sarah, described an elderly nun who regularly appeared during her shifts, disappearing always in the same place. 'There are more ghosts than staff,' she said. 'Pity we can't get them to do a few shifts.'

These very pressures might also shed some light on the question of why so many nurses feel they are benignly haunted all their working lives. Nurses deal with death on a daily basis, which might put them in the optimum posi-tion to catch sight of any lingering spirits, given how many of us will breathe our last breath in their workplaces. Perhaps more importantly, though, nurses must also deal with *life*. When a terminally ill patient enters a hospital to pass their final months in the greatest degree of comfort possible, it is the nurses who toil ceaselessly to ensure this happens. It is nurses who will grow fond of and familiar with their charges, learning the particular cadences of a patient's nocturnal cough, feeling a sense of emptiness when a favourite patient passes away. In a profession such as this one, it seems natural that to hear that nocturnal cough again might be a comfort easily imagined in the small hours, in the dark – and equally true that a nurse would know that Mary's cough was Mary's cough, even if Mary had since been transported to the morgue.

It isn't only nurses, however, who view the echoes of an older, less-understaffed past as a comfort in hospitals and care homes. My own father once told me that, one night in 2010 when my grandmother had been a patient at the Queen Elizabeth Hospital in Gateshead for several months following a stroke, he held open the door for a pleasant-faced woman in a ground-floor corridor whose cape and hat signalled reassurance – realising only belatedly that these were the accoutrements of a nurse of his own 1960s childhood, nothing the NHS would have allowed in the twenty-first century.

Meanwhile at her nursing home, one eighty-seven-year-old woman, Meg, accepted all the carers as a reassuring part of her daily routine: the day staff, the night staff – and the nun who wasn't there.

Meg's Nun

There's a way some people have of speaking to octogenarians as if they need to be handled carefully. I've always loathed it. Some of my favourite people are over the age of eighty, and sharper than others half their age. Nobody would have dared to speak to Meg like a child.

Physically frail, a care home had become a necessity for her, but she never forgot a word said to her and spent her afternoons industriously completing crossword puzzles, something she had once been told could stave off dementia. When others in the home began to decline mentally, she advocated for them. When she insisted on having a front room, first floor, so she could see who was coming and going, she got it. And when she expressed anything to the staff, they believed her. Meg was a battleaxe, an older

264

sister who'd assumed a 'take charge' air in her youth and never relinquished it.

Meg died some years ago, but this story isn't solely hers. It was told to me by her nephew, but it belonged to him, to Meg, and to the people who cared for her. The thing is, Meg might have been the first to see the nun, but she certainly wasn't the last.

It first came up one evening when Jim, then in his fifties, dropped in after work to visit his aunt on the way home. They were a close family; the care home had been Meg's own idea, preferable in her mind to being stowed in a younger relative's boxroom, as she put it. Her own house, with its stairs, had become impractical, so here she was, gazing out of the window from her perfect vantage point, watching visitors in the car park come and go.

It was late summer, still gloriously light at seven in the evening, but Jim still laughed at the sight of Meg so poised and watchful. 'There you are,' he said, tossing his blazer over the coat rack and approaching Meg in her wheelchair. 'All quiet on the Western Front?'

Meg turned towards him with a wry smile. 'No, as you'd see if you looked. A lot of commotion tonight.'

'Is it really that interesting?'

Meg was very often at the window when Jim arrived. He couldn't quite see what she took from it, a woman who still loved to read and knit and sew and inject her opinion into whatever conversation she could find. But Meg only shook her head, as if he was wilfully failing to understand.

'You can see a lot of things from this window,' she said. 'They think we don't know when someone's died, but I see the ambulance arriving. I know who's visiting who, and who doesn't come anymore. And I like to watch for my nun, of course.'

Jim blinked. He wondered whether he'd misheard. 'Your – nun?'

'My nun,' said Meg. 'Every night at nine o'clock, she walks down there' – Meg indicated the winding pathway that led across the front of the garden, just beyond the small car park – 'and sits on that bench. I hate to miss her.'

Jim was confused. Meg had always had a very dry sense of humour. As a child, he'd sometimes fallen foul of it, once spending an afternoon uselessly looking for 'sky hooks' after she'd told him, straight-faced, he'd find them if he only kept watching the clouds for long enough. He said, 'Is this one of your jokes?'

'No,' Meg said, mildly, and began to wheel herself away from the window. 'Come later one night and you'll see her. Shall we play cards?'

They played – Meg won, as she always did – and then it was dinner time, and time for Jim to be getting home, but as he drove, he turned their conversation over thoughtfully in his mind. Had Meg been pulling his leg? It was devilishly hard to tell.

It was some weeks before the subject came up again. Jim didn't dare to broach it, and Meg seemed absolutely unconcerned about it. Then, one Thursday in October,

Jim's daughter's school had a parents' evening which meant he'd had to dash there immediately after work, disrupting his usual schedule. He could have passed on his visit to Meg, but he wasn't inclined to. Thursday was their day, and Meg wouldn't mind if he turned up late.

By the time he got to the care home, it was after nine. Past visiting hours, but he was a sufficiently familiar face that he was granted permission just to dash up and give Meg a hug and his apologies. When he opened Meg's door, he was surprised to see her still at the window, although darkness had almost completely settled over the gardens below.

Meg turned towards him and laughed. 'Oh, Jim, you've just missed her.'

'I've – what?' asked Jim, disorientated.

'Missed her,' said Meg patiently. 'The nun. I told you: nine o'clock, she walks along there, and sits on the bench. And then she disappears.' Meg settled back into her wheel-chair with a sigh, as if Jim were a particularly irritating child. 'I suppose you can close the curtains.'

When Jim left, fifteen minutes later, he must have looked pensive, because one of Meg's carers stopped him on the stairs to ask whether everything was all right.

'Oh,' Jim said, 'yes – well. Meg's all right, I think, but she's mentioned something weird. Has she had a – I mean, does she need a—?'

The words 'cognitive assessment' stuck in his throat like a betrayal. The carer seemed to realise, because she smiled slightly nervously and then said, 'The nun?'

'Yes,' Jim said at once, seizing upon this gratefully. 'She's said it twice now, about this nun that comes at the same time every day. I don't know what to make of it. She's always had a strange sense of humour, but it seems . . .'

He stopped. The carer touched his arm gently and said, 'Come into the office. Let's talk.'

Like most visitors, Jim had never been into The Office before. Mounted on the wall were a number of security cameras, showing views of the care home from various angles. One of them, Jim now saw, focused clearly on the bench allegedly so beloved by the nun. Jim frowned, then looked to the carer for an explanation.

She was, evidently, slightly embarrassed. Delicately, she said, 'Meg started to mention this nun to us a few months ago. We thought the same as you – first of all, that she was having a little joke. And then we thought maybe we should get her an assessment.'

Jim could only imagine how that had gone. 'Right,' he said. 'And she said—?'

The carer cleared her throat. 'Well,' she admitted, 'she said she'd have the assessment *on condition* that a member of my staff came first to sit with her at nine o'clock, and look for herself.'

Jim's throat felt thick. 'And?' he pushed.

The carer tried to shrug unconcernedly. It was rather a failed attempt. 'And she saw her. The nun. Walking across the path, and then sitting on the bench, just like Meg said. A minute later she'd vanished. So . . .'

Jim could hear the blood rushing in his ears, a rather dizzying feeling. 'And – well, I mean – what if they're both just in on it? It could be – she could be—'

The carer laid a hand gently on Jim's arm once more. She took a deep breath, and then said, 'I've seen it as well, Mr Gibson. Not from upstairs, but after what my nurse said, I worried we had some sort of pervert lurking about. I watched on the camera, there.'

She pointed. Jim looked and then said, slightly hysterically, 'And?'

'And I saw the nun,' said the carer. 'She walked down the path, and she sat on the bench, and then she disappeared. I saw it plain as day, and then when we changed tapes, I went through to find it again, just to have another look.' She looked Jim dead in the eye. 'And it wasn't on the recording. I went through hours and hours in case I had the wrong timestamp, but it just wasn't there.' She bit her lip. 'If you want to, of course, we can still send Meg for the assessment. But—'

'No,' said Jim at once. Suddenly he wanted very much to get out of the care home. 'She – she seems to like watching for her, so she says. It's . . . her routine. And if you don't think she's losing it . . .'

'No,' admitted the carer. 'Unless we all are. I thought my staff might get antsy if it got out, but they don't seem to mind it. Meg's so calm about it.'

'She always is,' Jim said.

*

Comfort is more often a part of ghost belief than one might imagine. The Victorians associated ghost stories with Christmastime, a gloomy period of the year when the whole community was offered a rare chance to come together. Telling ghost stories was not only enlivening, but a bonding experience, the sharing of shivers and secrets in the dark. In the same way, nurses pass on ghost stories almost as an initiation ritual: having become part of the community, new recruits are introduced not only to the matrons and consultants, but also to the spirits they too might one day see. The exchange of such tales is also, of course, a welcome distraction in the witching hour, when the darkness of a ward, filled with the gentle sounds of machines and midnight breathing, might seem mesmeric. Ghost stories spike our adrenaline, keep us awake. They might also make our eyes just slightly more inclined to identify humanoid shapes in the dark.

Beyond the idea of a distraction, however, the Grey Nurse phenomenon reveals perhaps another crucial element of why so many of us remain keen to believe. To nurses convinced that a sister from the past has lulled a patient to sleep or helped avert a medical catastrophe, these beings are not so much spooks as safety blankets. Who wouldn't want to feel that an unseen hand will be there to catch our impending mistakes and stop us from making them? For the Cornish miners who took their trade to the USA, the presence of *coblynau* and knockers offered such comfort that they refused to work without them: their lights served as stark warnings, and miners' belief in them saved many lives – whether they ever existed or not. For nurses, the Grey Nurse offers something of the same thing – an assurance that someone will catch you before you fall, or perhaps come back to console you in a time of professional grief. The Grey Nurse is a vital reassertion of community spirit, not only among living nurses, but stretching back, too, to those who came before, and forward to those who will come after. In her way, she offers an assurance that we go on, and that things that were once important to us will remain so.

In the UK, there are certainly public hauntings which are closer to public nuisances, and our unquenchable desire to be frightened means that spectres of this sort can generate a huge pull – and subsequently, a huge payday for whoever operates the most successful ghost tour. It's easy to dismiss these hauntings as falling into an entirely different category from mundane spectral drinkers and students who never leave the classroom. In reality, however, belief in them still serves the same sort of purpose.

At Oxford Castle, one would-be ghost hunter, Lauren, reported feeling suddenly sick in a room which, so said the tour operator, was known to contain a malevolent spirit. Within moments, those around her, formerly strangers, said the same. By the time the tour was over, a group of six women who'd clutched at and jumped with each other for an hour were exchanging phone numbers, bound by the adrenaline rush into a strong sense of togeth-erness. War makes strong bonds, they say; but so, perhaps, do ghost tours – where the enemy may be imagined, but the effect is the same.

Ghosts and ghost belief shape and reshape our communities, whether the spirit is accepted as part of the in-crowd or feared as an outsider against whom to feel united. Unthreatening stories of footsteps on the stairs and soldiers in the cellar can offer a sense of togetherness in the telling, but they also serve as a comforting indicator that, whatever and whoever we are, we have always been and will always be. As we lean against the bar and down a final pint at our local, perhaps the sudden appearance of a compatriot from centuries ago might spook us – but on some level, it's a pleasing thought, that perhaps one can always come back. Perhaps we *can* go home again. Drink up.

And in the End . . .

IN THE INTRODUCTION TO this book, I pondered: what are the things that haunt us – and are these things the same, from one community to the next? Can the similarity in our spectres, from the *munaciello* of Naples to the Cornish redcap, the banshee to *la llorona* – be explained by widespread shared anxieties?

On a basic level, I feel the answer to this must be 'yes'. Despite differences in our individual circumstances, all human beings are dogged by similar concerns. As I wrote this book, the idea of community repeatedly centred itself in the stories I explored, particularly as an in-group which therefore defines what lies outside of it. Belonging and unbelonging; fear and protection – these are things which lie at the root of our ghost stories the world over.

As communities, it's natural to see the same anxieties repeatedly recur, whatever our position in time or space.

We fear invaders, and invasion. Specifically, we fear an attack on our children, whether by an interloper lurking within the community, or by an intruder from without. Connected to this is the horror of any rebellion against the status quo, like that which propelled the wild fervour of the Witch Trials and continues to fuel misogyny today. We wonder, too, where we fit in the world, nervous of ever finding ourselves on the outside of the in-group – and this leads us to ponder what happens after we die. Where will we go then? Will we still belong? Or will we find ourselves in one of those unreachable spaces, the uncharted Above or the worrisome Below, which are also the subjects of many a ghost story?

As the stories in this book have indicated, people approach these concerns in remarkably similar fashions, wherever we are from. Undeniably, our belief in witches reflects a lingering anxiety about social misfits, and the damage they might do to the community if left unchecked. Usefully, however – whether the witches we believe in are flesh and blood spell casters or their lingering ghosts – a witch can be resisted. Our reactions to witches, and our enduring superstitions around things like rowan trees, horseshoes and witch bottles, reflect our hope that a defence against spiritual pests is possible. A witch can be resisted, and a community can survive beyond her.

Wider ghost belief, in some ways, is also connected to the idea of community survival. In the last chapter, we considered some public spectres, many of whom provided the reassuring idea that even in death, we may not be

274

forced to find a new and less convivial pub to drink in. When our work is difficult or dangerous, we may not be alone in it, if those who went before us remain to keep a watchful eye. And, when a spectre *is* malevolent or frightening, its presence only serves to bind us more tightly together, united once more against an invasive outsider. Our tendency to populate the worrying Above and Below with intercessors – placing ghosts in school attics and basements; hearing the steps of Victorian track walkers still following the rails beneath London – is another way these stories reassure us. Life goes on. The empty spaces are not empty. You will never be alone, a thought that soothes and unsettles in equal parts.

Telling ghost stories is a beloved pastime the world over, whether those ghosts are really believed in or not. And as the stories in this book indicate, although many of our stories adhere to broad archetypes, they are also often specific, local variations, whose characteristics mean they simply could not have appeared anywhere else. Our ghosts grow out of our communities, then feed back into them in a process of constant iteration shaped by local culture, geography and history. A White Lady in rural Northumberland can only ever be, at best, a distant cousin of her central London ghost walk counterpart. Ghost stories twist in the telling, and the spirit in which they are told can have a significant effect. Sometimes, a story brewed in a bottle, in isolation, will develop a potency that's lost when, in other instances, a tale is too often exposed to the light.

All communities, by nature of simply being social units, are focused on togetherness, protecting the in-group and resisting the out-group. But it's clear that the specific histories and geographies of communities also loom large in their modern existences and change not only the way they believe, but the things they believe in. Writing in the *Financial Times*, the geographer Nick Middleton described a journey through Central America along a 'line of volcanoes punched through the landscape, vents to the underworld that explain many attributes of the culture, history and traditions of the region.' The volcanoes he describes have resulted in more dramatic and destructive tectonic shifts than anything we have seen in the UK, but the powerful connection between geography and culture is equally identifiable in some of the stories in this book. In Chapter Four, I used the city of Naples as an example, detailing how its position atop a deeply cut subterranean kingdom has shaped its culture, its history – and its ghosts. Certain areas of the UK have long been thought of as 'closer to' the spirit world, having a more pragmatic and more enduring belief in ghosts than some of their neighbouring counties. It's no surprise, then, that many of these areas have similarly marked geographical features which have affected not only their history in industry, but also their modern culture as 'former' mining areas.

From the slate mines of mountainous Wales, to shaft-ridden Northumberland, to the tin seams of Cornwall and beyond, the mining history of certain parts of the UK has also led to ongoing and entrenched belief in protective spirits, shifting with the times and yet never eradicated. So powerful was this cultural belief in the case of the Cornish that their underground companions travelled with them across the Atlantic to the USA: the Cornish were miners, and no mine could be thought safe without its knockers. The fact that the Californian mines produced the same physical phenomena that confirmed the presence of knockers in Cornwall merely cemented the connection.

At the same time, just as the geography and history of an area can shape its hauntings, so too can a known haunting shape an area – sometimes in the most unexpected and enduring way. The haunted house in Elspeth Street was one of the first hauntings of which I became aware, and drove my research into ghost belief more widely. What intrigued me about it was how far the ripples of that haunting were felt, even before the details of the story itself were clear to me. The notoriety of this haunting has had real-world effects on the housing market; the knowledge of this private home being reputedly haunted is also used as an initiation into the local community, the in-group.

In the same way, the stark figure of the Spooky House at Craig Y Mor haunts the local area through its notoriety, even in the absence of any particular spectre-in-residence. Its existence compels locals and visitors alike. It shapes the childhoods of those who grew up in its shadow, and causes the uninitiated to sketch imaginary spectres into its nooks and crannies. The Spooky House is, to an extent, inhabited, but it often doesn't feel so. As a society, we dislike the thought of a purpose-built place becoming abandoned: we feel so haunted by the emptiness of abandoned places that the concept of their being inhabited by ghosts is almost comforting, even while it sends a chill down the spine.

Our ghosts, and the ways in which we understand and believe in them, are shaped by time as well as distance. In many instances, it seems that modern supernatural belief is serving the same purpose as it did two hundred, five hundred, or even a thousand years ago. Children avoid the woods at night because they fear a witch's sinister ghost lurking within them; this witch, whether she exists or not, therefore protects them from the physical dangers by which they might set less store. Many teenagers feel they are invincible in the face of trip hazards and tramps, but the threat of a witch like Cuckoo Nanny, in the area where I grew up, will make them wary. In other instances, however, we can see that the same phenomena can remain at the core of supernatural belief, while the way these phenomena are interpreted is hugely altered by social and historical context.

Ritchie, and his brushes with knockers, is a case in point. Ritchie, and many other former miners I spoke to, confirmed that the mining industry remained rife with spiritual co-workers well into the twenty-first century. It makes sense that, operating miles below the earth in a hinterland space often utterly black, a flare of blue light or the creaking of metal will draw as much attention today as they would have hundreds of years ago. The spirits that attend miners serve as warnings and promises: they indicate seams to investigate, and areas to avoid, and they are usually right. However, the miners of the twenty-first century are not operating within the same cultural context as their ancestors. Those who believed in bluecaps and *coblynau* were still steeped in stories of the Fair Folk, the green-tinged mischievous beings whose realm lay beneath our feet and whose whims could be treacherous. Ritchie and his co-workers brought their modern mindset under-ground with them, and consequently parsed the lights and footsteps in a different way, as ghosts rather than goblins. Similarly, the mine operators of California were willing to accept the fact of the presence of knockers, but hadn't the cultural context to view them as fairy kin. Knockers endure, but they have reshaped themselves as necessary so that they may continue to do the job they were devised to do, in any cultural context.

Forever evolving to serve us better, today's underground spirits usually take the shape of fallen colleagues, long-dead miners come back to prevent those who come after from suffering the fate that killed them. Likewise, the ghosts of the Underground that offer signals and solace to railway staff are interpreted as being the spirits of deceased workers, still and forever members of the community. They may be frightening, but they are also comprehensible in the way that a goblin or a fairy no longer could be. For us, fairies are a thing of the past, but the lights and shadows once attributed to them are not. No matter – we simply transform them into something else.

In a less extreme way, the same thing has happened to the witches of the British Isles. In Chapter Three, I discussed how many of the same anxieties that led seventeenth-century witch prickers like John Kincaid to launch intensive witch-hunts are still abroad here. We still castigate, cancel and publicly humiliate our witches, those individuals we feel to be stepping out of line. We may no longer hang them, but ostracisation remains a key tool in our arsenal. Where once a rude or unobliging woman might have been charged with witchcraft, now those who deviate from 'normal' behaviour or beliefs might find themselves bullied off social media at best, or falsely accused of a crime at worst, as in the days of the 'Satanic panic' of the 1980s and 1990s. Propelled by the religious right, some twelve thousand accusations of child sexual abuse and Satanic 'cult' behaviour were levelled in the United States; not a single investigation uncovered any evidence. The moral panic still took years to die down – albeit, thankfully, it didn't have the staying power of the original witch trials. Still, moral panics arise with predict-able regularity, and every one is essentially a witch-hunt. As in the seventeenth century, the idea of being unable to resist a witch petrifies us. It's just that we've slightly redefined who our witches are.

The 'witch' of the twenty-first century has been split into several elements, whereas once upon a time, all of these could be found together. Today, we like to say we no longer believe in magic, but even if some people deride modern covens as 'New Age nonsense', part of us still fears what they might be up to – what they might stir up. In the same way, the witches of previous centuries still cast long shadows over us. For the most part, we accept that the unfortunate women hanged as witches were only human, incapable of curses or spells. But what if our ancestors' witch bottles worked? What if the witches' souls are trapped in our houses? And what if they really *were* witches, after all? There are certain pockets of the United Kingdom where witch fervour was rife; it's not surprising that ongoing witch belief and witch anxiety remains strongest in those areas, driven by the continued discovery of shoes, stoppered bottles and all the other traps our ancestors set. Their past continues to intrude upon, inhabit and reshape our present. Best to put the shoe back up the chimney, where it belongs. Just in case. Why do we continue to believe so powerfully in things which, our educated minds tell us, are utterly irrational? Often, 'just in case' seems to be the only true answer.

*

When you live, as I do, in the middle of nowhere, any journey can carry you over hill and dale, down the deep lanes of the North Cotswolds and even past the odd mesolithic-stone-circle-turned-New-Age-pilgrimage-site. One recent morning, as I turned out of Little Rollright and onto the long, narrow road flanked by the King's Stone on one side and his Men and Knights on the other, a familiar brown heritage sign leaped out at me. The Rollright Stones. I stopped.

I opened the little wooden kissing gate, deposited my nominal entrance fee in the little metal box and headed to the right, towards the irregular circle of stones known as the King's Men. Legend has it that these lumps of pitted oolitic limestone were once an army – until they had the misfortune to encounter a witch. The witch told the King that if, after seven strides, he could see Long Compton in the distance, he would be King of all England – but, as with most witchy promises, the terms and conditions were ill-defined. At the last moment, a great mound rose up, obscuring the King's view of the nearby village, and the witch turned them all to stone, every last man. The King became the King Stone, and his knights the Whispering Knights. The army became the King's Men. The witch, it is said, still lingers in the form of an elder tree which, if cut down, will break the spell, returning the stones to their fleshly forms. Given that a number of the King's Men have been pilfered over the years for use in local houses, barns and bridges, this would doubtless generate widespread alarm should it ever come to pass. So far, so good. The original witch, one elder tree among countless, remains in hiding.

Originally, of course, the witch was the villain of this story. Now, though, standing in the grass between the kissing gate and the stone circle, there is an eerily evocative wicker sculpture erected in her image. Various offerings – coins, crystals, a toffee or two – have been thrown into the circle of her skirts, as if requesting her assistance. The witch is a symbol of intentional power. Surely, if she can keep an army entombed in stone for thousands of years, any other request would be child's play to her?

The circle of the King's Men itself is, today, a place for offerings. Some would describe it as 'New Age-y' and, indeed, some of the brightly coloured ribbons and woven Brigid's squares suggest the forethought and determined intention of a Wiccan practitioner (or at least dabbler). But others – the small piles of stones made upon larger ones; the coins tucked into nooks and crannies in the rock – are less 'determined intention', more 'why not?' As I examined the offerings (good luck to Ken and Carlin, who inscribed their names on a heart and hung it up to protect their love) I noticed a man making his way around the periphery of the stone circle in a nervous fashion, as if hoping not to be noticed. With each stone he passed, he laid his palm atop it and his mouth shaped a soundless word. Anyone who had read the helpful fixed signage would have known what he was doing. *The King's Men are famously Uncountable! If you can count them three times and get the same number, you can have any wish you like.*

I don't think this man stopped off at the Rollright Stones hoping for a wish to be granted. Equally, I imagine that if anyone had approached him to ask what he was doing, the process would have been dismissed as a bit of fun, a nonsense. He didn't want to be seen courting wishes, and yet here he was, laboriously doing it. The thing is, in a place like this, it's difficult to stop oneself surrendering to the impulse. You don't have to believe in the witch and the curse to feel the centuries of intention shimmering in the air, pulsing in the gaps between stones. A site of New Age pilgrimage this may now be, but it's also a reflection of one of the oldest desires of all – to come together with other people and believe in something until it manifests. What has survived about the Rollright Stones is not the misfortune that befell the King, but the memory of the witch's success, and some level of hope that we, too, could share in it, if we only commit to the bit. Walk the circle, leave the offering. Hope for the best, and genuflect vaguely out of fear of what might happen if you don't.

Before I returned to my car, I tipped the witch's sculpture a penny – just in case.

*

This book is about ghosts and the ways in which, in the twenty-first century, we still believe in them. Perhaps more accurately, though, it is about *hauntings*. In Britain, as elsewhere, we are haunted by supernatural beliefs and superstitions harking back to our earliest ancestors, the light of their ancient beliefs now refracted through our own modern lens. The beliefs of thousands of years ago have shaped our modern landscapes: not only in the form of stone circles, but also in the way the countryside burns red with rowan trees in season, and our churchyards are shadowed by protective yews.

In researching this book, one of the things that most struck me was that the same places endure through time as homes for our societal hopes and fears – be that the underground world, the remote and secret lair of the presumed witch, or the abandoned building. We may not always populate these places with exactly the same characters, or ascribe to them the same meanings, but the intentions of our predecessors are inscribed upon them almost, indeed, as if they were Stone Tapes – and the idea of disregarding those intentions frightens us in a superstitious way. What better example could we have of this than the neolithic monuments which, like the Uffington White Horse, we still clean, or the pocketed standing stones to which we still pay obeisance, even without knowing why? Centuries of belief leave too powerful a mark to be quickly erased. Their aftermath niggles at us, even if the idea of being caught trekking three times round a stone circle fills us with sheepish embarrassment.

Joseph Rhodes Buchanan, who coined the term 'psychometry' in 1842, wrote: 'The Past is entombed in the Present! The world is its own enduring monument; and that which is true of its physical, is likewise true of its mental career.' I may not believe in psychometry, but I cannot argue with his central thesis. Its evidence is all around us.

*

I noted in the introduction to this book that the identity of our spectres and spooks is often not important. The stories I've collected seem to bear this out. Occasionally, such as in the case of White Ladies or other 'community ghosts', some identity or other has been mooted as the root of the spiritual disturbance. In such cases, our interpretation of that character has often changed through time, as in the case of Mary Eleanor Bowes of Gibside – a wild and radical woman in her own time, and a member of the nobility; in her modern form, lauded for her self-possession and accepted as part of the very community she once lorded over. In most cases, however, the spirits we whisper about are disembodied in the most literal way. The bodies they once inhabited are not important. Their significance is in their afterlives, and the ways in which these intersect with our lived existences.

Our ghosts unite us, not because of who they are, but because of who *we* are. When a trusted friend, colleague or family member shares with us the story of their midnight brush with a spook on the stairs, a vulnerable hand is extended. There is no logic, no rhyme or reason, to ghosts. We all know this. But to offer a story is to step into the unknown; to risk ridicule; to proffer a fresh bond for forging. In some places – in some community groups; within some industries; in some parts of the country – it's an easier step to take than in others. In all cases, however, when we give up our ghosts, we are saying: you may not believe a stranger, but believe me. Believe me – and the community will go on.

While supernatural belief in the British Isles and beyond has certainly changed over time – and varies widely – it has not gone away. The world may be changing at a faster pace than ever before, but the same urges drive us, the same fears dog us. Accordingly, through our enduring superstitions and supernatural beliefs, we often handle them in the same ways as our ancestors might have, albeit adapted to a context we can better understand. This context might be shaped by our community's history, by its geography, by its culture; the community itself might be determined by the area in which we live, or it might be our profession, class, religion or upbringing. Ultimately, however, ghosts, like the global economy or the placebo effect, exist because we believe in them. If the contents of this book are any indication, this seems unlikely to change any time soon.

In 2023, the BBC broadcast a documentary series, *Paranormal: The Ghost, the Girl and the Gravestone*. In it, Radio 1 DJ Sian Eleri is seen trekking through North Wales, seeking to unravel the mystery of what was once dubbed 'the most haunted house in Britain'. Penyffordd Farm was a site of national interest when, in the 1990s, the resident Gower family claimed to have experienced more than three hundred apparitions and manifestations, chief among them being ghostly writing on the wall. Eleri's investigation – and the speed at which her scepticism falls away – is interesting; but what struck me most was a moment when, 'off-duty', she questions a number of young people taking a smoke break outside a club in a busy city street. They're trendily dressed; they're modern youth. When Eleri explains what she's doing in Wales, they laugh and say, self-deprecatingly, 'I don't really believe in ghosts – but, well . . .'

And then they tell their stories. The whispers they've heard in the night; the strange apparitions they've heard about from family members or friends. We might say we don't *really* believe in ghosts, but once somebody else is brave enough to admit that they do – well, then, the stories come out; the caveats dwindle away. The scene made me smile because it reflected so closely what I've found in my own research, as I mentioned this book to friends and colleagues who laughed, and then – shyly, eagerly – told me their own stories. Everybody, or almost everybody, has a ghost story. All we need is somebody we trust to listen to it.

Some people in the twenty-first century seem to view their interest in paranormal spirits as an embarrassing habit. Furtively, secretly, they subscribe to podcasts like *Unexplained* or *Ghost Story* and hope nobody will ever ask what they listen to on the treadmill. They watch *Uncanny* on catch-up, alone in the dark, and minimise the screen when a spouse enters. In some ways, then, I've found it helpful to meet people where they are, and out myself first as a fellow indulger: 'Hello, I'm Jay and I love ghost stories. This is a safe space.' The sense of spreading relief is always palpable. Now they can admit to their preoccupation with reincarnated children, or cursed objects; now, they can mention the unsettling event in their past which has long defied explanation, and occupied more space in the mind than it rightly deserves. I love ghost stories, and I believe in ghosts. It's all right. Lots and lots of us do.

For all the stories in this book which were told to me enthusiastically and without prompting, there is another which came when I least expected it, from a person I would never have imagined to have even a passing interest in the paranormal. In many ways, these – such as Sophie's haunted shoe shop, or the oven which terrified George by continually turning itself on – are my favourites. I like them because they remind me that ghost stories are a fundamental part of all of us, whether or not we want them to be. Sometimes, the most sceptical of upbringings does little to quell the fact that, like Fox Mulder, part of us wants to believe. More than that, we want to *be* believed.

Speaking to the *Guardian* in 2021, Danny Robins, creator of the podcast-turned-television show *Uncanny*, suggested that his parents' atheism was in fact the catalyst for his lifelong obsession with ghosts. 'I think I might have just wanted to be part of a club,' he said. 'To be part of a club of believers.' Robins suggests that the recent meteoric rise of the horror podcast is tied to the isolation of the pandemic: ghost stories, he says, are 'a way to mitigate our fear . . . that our existence has been meaningless.' They act 'as a mirror, reflecting back the chaos and fear we feel.' It seems a reasonable position to take. The rise in spiritualism after the First World War was born of similar motivations, a reaction to devastating and monumental loss; who knows how many other points in the long and storied history of these isles have seen booms in paranormal preoccupation, a seismic trauma response? Ghosts are our past, our present and, perhaps, our future. What could be more natural than a fascination with that?

Hello. I'm Jay. I love ghost stories, and I believe in ghosts. I bet you do, too. Why don't you tell me yours?

Further Reading:
For Your Reference

Introduction

James, M. R., 'Oh, Whistle and I'll Come To You, My Lad' from *Ghost Stories of an Antiquary* (E Arnold, 1904).

Chapter One: House Guests

Mantel, Hilary, *Giving Up The Ghost: A Memoir* (Fourth Estate, 2003)

Chapter Two: White Ladies

Beardsley, Richard K. and Hankey, Rosalie (January 1943). 'A History of the Vanishing Hitchhiker'. *California Folklore Quarterly*. 2 (1): 13–25. doi:10.2307/1495651. JSTOR 1495651.

Brunvald, Jan Harold, *The Vanishing Hitchhiker: American Urban Legends and Their Meanings* (W. W. Norton, 1981)

Moore, Wendy, *Wedlock: How Georgian Britain's Worst Husband Met His Match* (W&N, 2009)

https://www.theguardian.com/uk/gallery/2009/jan/09/tyrone-ghost

Chapter Three: Rumours of Witches

Bourn, William, *History of the Parish of Ryton* (G&T Coward, 1896)

Hutton, Ronald, *The Witch: A History of Fear, from Ancient Times to the Present* (Yale University Press, 2017)

Macdonald, Arthur, 'That Tring Air. A Gossiping and Irresponsible History of Tring, Hertfordshire' (1941) https://tringlocalhistory.org.uk/Tring_Air/index.htm

Needham, Rodney, *Primordial Characters* (University Press of Virginia, 1978)

https://mgscott.blogspot.com/2018/01/beyond-witches-circle-factfile-9-was.html?fbclid=IwAR1VhKdfT9UMr GWnVPoTsp4NrBBWmZpDmMIH_RP3K3pp CXPeac1EPcJEke0

https://www.ebooksread.com/authors-eng/william-bourn-of-whickham/history-of-the-parish-of-ryton-goo/page-15-history-of-the-parish-of-ryton-goo.shtml

https://northeastlore.com/2015/10/

https://www.grimsbytelegraph.co.uk/news/grimsby-news/mystery-behind-witches-circle-grimsby-4741179

https://www.satra.com/bulletin/article.php?id=2078

https://blackthornandstone.com/2020/09/02/witch-bottles-hidden-curses-objects-of-protection-objects-of-vengeance/

https://museumofwitchcraftandmagic.co.uk/object/curse-shoe/

Chapter Four: Underground

Long, Brian, *Presence in the Pit* (independently published)

On Naples:

https://faroutmagazine.co.uk/naples-saints-spirits-
    superstition-italy-city/

http://ilregno2s.blogspot.com/2011/08/the-little-monk-
    exploring-o-munaciello.html

https://random-times.com/2019/07/07/legends-and-
    origins-of-o-munaciello-the-neapolitan-sprite/

On miners:

https://www.edcgov.us/landing/Living/Stories/pages/
    tommyknockers.aspx

https://www.legendsofamerica.com/gh-tommyknockers/

King, Stephen, *The Tommyknockers* (Putnam, 1987)

Chapter Five: Private Property, Public Interest

https://www.orphandriftarchive.com/articles/hyperstition/

https://home.howstuffworks.com/real-estate/selling-
    home/haunted-house-for-sale.htm

https://www.walesonline.co.uk/lifestyle/welsh-homes/
    mysterious-spooky-house-thats-been-25521677

https://www.hauntedrooms.co.uk/newsham-park-hospital-
    liverpool

https://www.mirror.co.uk/news/uk-news/inside-uks-most-
    haunted-building-27467565

https://www.dailypost.co.uk/whats-on/arts-culture-news/
    secret-anglesey-16-forgotten-tales-16414579

https://www.liverpoolecho.co.uk/news/liverpool-news/
    ghosts-poltergeists-ufos-merseysides-most-25365049

https://www.liverpoolecho.co.uk/news/liverpool-news/
    former-worker-newsham-park-hospital-13074963

Chapter Six: A Public Spectacle

Laurent, Claire, *Myths and Rituals in Nursing: A Social History* (Pen & Sword History, 2019)

Schick, Theodore and Vaughan, Lewis, *How to Think About Weird Things: Critical Thinking for a New Age* (McGraw Hill, 2013)

https://www.hauntedhappenings.co.uk/george-jarvis-school/

https://yourherefordshire.co.uk/all/featured-articles/things-to-do-this-former-boarding-school-in-herefordshire-is-now-available-for-ghost-hunts-are-you-brave-enough/

https://www.walesonline.co.uk/news/education/ghost-primary-school-roath-cardiff-21911540#comments-wrapper

https://britishfairies.wordpress.com/2021/05/30/poor-little-greenie-faeries-and-little-green-men/

https://www.cheshire-live.co.uk/news/chester-cheshire-news/spine-tingling-haunted-happenings-one-13777666

https://hauntedhistoryoflincolnshire.blogs.lincoln.ac.uk/lincoln/the-lion-and-snake/

https://www.greeneking.co.uk/newsroom/latest-news/halloween-haunted-pub-guide-stories/

https://adelaidehauntedhorizons.com.au/grey-nurse-hospital-ghost/

https://rcni.com/nursing-standard/newsroom/analysis/spooky-stories-wards-why-do-so-many-nurses-have-one-183736

https://www.theguardian.com/tv-and-radio/2021/mar/29/fear-in-your-ear-horror-podcast-battersea-poltergeist

Acknowledgements

There are many people without whom this book would never have come to fruition. First of all, of course I must acknowledge all those who were willing to tell me their stories, the vast majority of whom I have anonymised in these pages. Thank you for your trust, your interest, and your good memories.

My agent, Sandra Sawicka at Marjacq Scripts, saw the potential in this book and helped enormously as I shaped it into a saleable form. My editor, Justine Taylor at Bonnier Books, was hugely encouraging about the book from the start, and I must thank her and all the team at Bonnier.

My partner, Athena Artuso, has read versions of this manuscript more times than I can count. She has proofread, edited, praised and critiqued it; and also prevented me from mentioning The Beatles too much. My dear friend Sophie Duncan has listened to me stress about this book for the better part of the last four years, and never complained. My parents-in-law Lynda and Angelo Artuso have also been very encouraging; and one of Lynda's stories features in this book.

I'm grateful to my lovely colleagues – Edwin Drummond; Jason Fiddaman; Stacey Kennedy; Lauren Mohammed;

Emily Perkins and Kiri-Ann Olney – for a great Christmas drinks session in December 2023 in which I collected no less than five new ghost stories, to my delight. Their continued enthusiasm has also been considerable and pleasing!

Thank you to The Lads – Al Heath, Tish Dalli-Wright, Sam Cooper, Lydia Burt, Andrea Mattinson, Helen Lockett and Sarah Parish – for putting up with regular Book Discussion, both in the group chat and on our Big Walks, and for being so encouraging. Thanks to Jav, MJ, MK, and MD for same, minus the Big Walks.

Thank you to my longtime friend, Liam Rayner, for his support and also for many more things; and also to Danielle Lynch and Colleen Robinson for being the Australian contingent of supporters. Colleen introduced me to The Gothic and the rest is history.

Last but by no means least, I want to thank my parents and my sister 'Elizabeth' for being so supportive of my writing during difficult times – and, you know, for everything else. I love you.

Readers of this book: I am of course very grateful to you too, and if I might make one final demand on your time, I'd be very pleased if you'd consider donating to the Motor Neurone Disease Association.